6191620

CH 1982 7/12

ASHDOWN, D.M.
Queen Victoria's
mother
£2.80

B/KEN

QUEEN VICTORIA'S MOTHER

QUEEN VICTORIA'S MOTHER

DULCIE M. ASHDOWN

ROBERT HALE & COMPANY . LONDON

© *Dulcie M. Ashdown* 1974
First published in Great Britain 1974

ISBN 0 7091 4339 7

Robert Hale & Company
63 Old Brompton Road
London SW7

PRINTED IN GREAT BRITAIN BY
CLARKE DOBLE & BRENDON LTD.
PLYMOUTH

CONTENTS

ILLUSTRATIONS

ACKNOWLEDGEMENTS

The author wishes to acknowledge with thanks the assistance and interest of her publisher, Mr John Hale; the staff of the Reading Room of the British Museum and of Colindale Newspaper Library; the Archivist, Doctor Oswald, and his secretary, at the Furstliche Leiningensche Archiv in Amorbach; the library staff of the Royal College of Physicians, London; and the Librarian of Balliol College, Oxford.

Especial thanks are due to Miss Gillian M. Huber who froze in the Colindale Library and sweltered in German trains, braving Amorbach's mosquitoes and Coburg's steep hill in enthusiastic pursuit of material for this biography.

Authorization to reprint quotations from published sources has been obtained, and such quotations are obtained from the following books, with the permission of their authors and publishers:

W. H. Allen and Company: Helen Cathcart, *The Royal Bedside Book* (1969)

The Bodley Head Ltd: H. Bolitho and W. Baillie (ed.), *Letters of Lady Augusta Stanley, 1849–63* (Howe, 1967)

Cambridge University Press: J. Firth, *The Case of Augustus D'Este* (1948); A. Aspinall (ed.), *Letters of George IV, 1812–30* (1938)

Jonathan Cape Ltd: H. Temperley (ed.), *Unpublished diary . . . of Princess Lieven* (1925); J. Richardson, *My Dearest Uncle* (1961); H. Bolitho and W. Baillie (ed.), *Later Letters of Lady Augusta Stanley, 1864–76* (1929)

Chatto and Windus Ltd: U. Pope-Hennessey, *Agnes Strickland* (1940)

Evans Brothers (Books) Ltd: R. Fulford (ed.), *Dearest Child* (1965)

Eyre and Spottiswood (Publishers) Ltd.: H. Bolitho (ed.), *Further Letters of Queen Victoria* (Thornton-Butterworth, 1938)

ACKNOWLEDGEMENTS

Robert Hale and Company: H. A. Albert, *Queen Victoria's Sister* (1967)

Longmans Group Ltd: H. Bolitho, *A Biographer's Notebook* (Longmans Green, 1950); H. Reeve (ed.), *Greville Memoirs* Longmans Green, 1874–7)

Macmillan, London and Basingstoke: D. Creston, *Youthful Queen Victoria* (1952); R. Fulford, *The Prince Consort* (1949); R. Fulford and L. Strachey (ed.), *Greville Memoirs* (1938); D. M. Stuart, *Mother of Victoria* (1941)

Frederick Muller Ltd: D. Duff, *Edward of Kent* (Stanley Paul, 1938)

John Murray (Publishers) Ltd: Princess Beatrice (ed.), *In Napoleonic Days* (1941); H. Maxwell (ed.), *Creevey Papers* (1904); Lord Dudley (ed.), *Palmerston-Lieven Correspondence, 1828–58* (1943); H. Wyndham (ed.), *Correspondence of Sarah Spencer, Lady Lyttelton, 1787–1870* (1912); Viscount Esher and A. C. Benson (ed.), *The Letters of Queen Victoria, 1826–61* (1907); K. von Jagow (ed.), *Letters of the Prince Consort, 1831–61* (1938); Viscount Esher (ed.), *The Girlhood of Queen Victoria* (1912); A. Kennedy (ed.), *My Dear Duchess* (1956); P. Lindsay, *Recollections of a Royal Parish* (1902); *Cornhill Magazine*, 1897 and 1937

James Nisbet and Company Ltd: D. F. Gurney, *The Childhood of Queen Victoria* (1901); W. W. Tulloch, *The Story of the Life of Queen Victoria* (1901)

Sidgwick and Jackson Ltd: M. Gillen, *The Prince and His Lady* (1970)

Weidenfeld and Nicolson Ltd: E. Longford, *Victoria R.I.* (1964)

The author wishes to acknowledge also the kind permission of His Grace the Duke of Wellington, M.V.O., O.B.E., M.C., to quote from *A Selection from the Private Correspondence of the first Duke of Wellington*, published by the Roxburghe Club (1952).

Permission to quote from the manuscript journal of Lord Augustus d'Este was given by the Harveian Librarian of the Royal College of Physicians; extracts from the papers of Sir John Conroy are reproduced by permission of the Master and Fellows of Balliol College, Oxford.

To lose a beloved mother is always terrible, and the blank can never be filled, that you know. But when you consider that this mother has lived for no one and nothing but me, that for 41 years I have never been separated from her for more than three months, that she was the gentlest, most tender and loving creature that one can ever imagine, and that her heart, like none other, was always full of loving kindness for outside people, then you can imagine how immeasurable is my loss and my grief! May God be praised that my beloved mother fell gently asleep, and that even in her death her dear hand was clasped in mine!

Queen Victoria to Crown Princess Augusta of Prussia 27.3.61
(Bolitho (ed.), *Further Letters of Queen Victoria*, pp. 117–18)

INTRODUCTION

Countless biographies of Queen Victoria have been written, but only one has been devoted to the life of her mother.* Yet Victoire of Saxe-Coburg-Saalfeld, Duchess of Kent, is a fascinating character, little deserving the relative obscurity in which she has been left.

Her position itself would make the woman interesting: daughter of a petty German duke, wife of an even lesser princeling, then wife and widow in quick succession of one of George III's eccentric sons; mother of the heiress to the English crown and potential regent; a background figure in the key events of the troubled early years of her daughter's reign, and finally a close confidante of the remarkable ruler of a great nation. Her situation alone would set her apart—even had she not brought to it her deep and seemingly paradoxical character.

Queen Victoria's mother has often been portrayed as a hard, grasping, ambitious Jezebel—she would certainly appear so from the opinions of some contemporaries. She is known for her scheming to gain the regency for her daughter's minority, for her dubious relationship with Sir John Conroy and for the pressure she put on her daughter tirelessly for years in order to maintain her own authority over her. Few biographers of the Queen pass over the fact that immediately upon attaining the throne, she removed herself from her mother's bed and company, began a routine of cool aloofness from her and relied instead on a substitute mother, her former governess, Baroness Lehzen.

Yet one still has to reconcile this picture with the warmth of the mother-daughter relationship of the 1840s and 1850s, and

* D. M. Stuart, *Mother of Victoria* (Macmillan, 1941).

with the sincerity of Queen Victoria's grief at the Duchess's death in 1861. Her vociferous praise of her mother at that time is in direct contrast with the condemnation of her in the royal diaries of 1837–40.

One problem which biographers have always had to face in appraising Victoire, Duchess of Kent (it was only in the 1830s that she adopted the more familiar form of the name, 'Victoria') is the lack of evidence, the want of her own recorded motives and opinions, the sparsity of accessible material on the Duchess in her private life. Too many have relied on the comments of contemporary observers with an axe to grind against her. Only recently have English sources revealed the formerly obscure period of her early life in Germany and the circumstances of her marriage to Edward, Duke of Kent.

It is time that a re-appraisal was made of the character of Queen Victoria's mother, giving new lights on her life—as far as still-lacking material permits. As a formative influence on such a historical giant as her daughter, Queen Victoria, the Duchess of Kent will essentially remain a controversial—but will perhaps emerge as a more credible—personality.

CHAPTER ONE

In Coburg and Amorbach

Queen Victoria's mother was Victoire Marie Louise, youngest daughter of Francis and Augusta of Saxe-Coburg-Saalfeld. She was born on 17th August 1786 in the town of Coburg which was the 'capital' of the dukedom then ruled by her grandfather. Her birthday fell on an inauspicious date: Frederick the Great, King of Prussia, founder of the fortunes of the House of Hohenzollern, the German hero of his age, had died on the very day on which Victoire entered the world. It was a coincidence which was slightly to mar her childhood birthdays, for her grandmother, whose sister had been the wife of Frederick the Great, would never allow her birthday to be celebrated on a day which was devoted to the memories of her illustrious brother-in-law.

The old Duchess Sophia Antoinette felt that she had some reason to play up her relationship with royalty, for her own alliance with the House of Coburg was scarcely one to boast of—in her opinion. However, to its own members, the family was one to be proud of. It was one of a group of Saxon Houses which had ruled in the area known as Franconia for some five hundred years. Indeed, its great medieval castle, the 'Veste', set on the hill above the town, was known as 'the crown of Franconia', and could boast of having sheltered Martin Luther, the reformer, during the early days of the continental Reformation. Such associations would mean little, however, to the Duchess, whose only ambition was to make her court equal in magnificence to those of her superiors. To this end, she spent lavishly—to the impoverishment of her husband's estates, and by the end of the eighteenth century found herself forced into a necessity of humiliating financial retrenchment.

The proud Duchess's grandchildren therefore knew what it was to have to scrimp and save. Their father, Francis, the Duke's heir, lived in the Schloss Ehrenburg in the town—as it were, in the shadow of the ducal couple who occupied the ancient Schloss on the hill. Schloss Ehrenburg had been built in the more prosperous days of the seventeenth century, and had more recent additions, but with purses now tightening, it was beginning to look shabby, and to need repairs. With seven children— Ernest, Ferdinand, Leopold, Antoinette, Sophia, Juliana and Victoire—to clothe, feed and educate, money was scarce, and the Coburgs of the 1780s would consider themselves poor in comparison with neighbouring aristocrats. Indeed, the only anecdote of Victoire's childhood to have come down to us highlights the family's poverty: a little girl from the town, Christina Stockmar, came sometimes to play at the Schloss, and was shocked one day to find the little Princess Antoinette in tears over a torn frock; it was her 'Sunday' frock, and she had no replacement. Christina was begged to help mend the dress before Antoinette's mother saw the damage.

Christina Stockmar was fondest of the Princess Victoire. "for her amiability and her many pranks",[1] but there can have been little time for romps and play after her days of infancy. The prime object of aristocratic parents was to train their daughters for marriage—a marriage which would bring credit to their own House. Thus, while Europe watched the turmoil of the French Revolution, in the quiet of Coburg, Victoire had to concentrate on acquiring a little learning and, more important, the practicalities of household management, and the arts and accomplishments which would while away the leisure hours of her maturity.

In 1796, a red-letter occasion brightened the child's routine of study and work, with the marriage of her sister Juliana to the Grand Duke Constantine of Russia. It was an amazing piece of good fortune for the family, a match out of all proportion to their expectations—but then the Romanovs could afford to overlook the sparsity of the Coburg dowry; they had gained great tsarinas from unequal matches with minor German Houses, and might expect to do so again. The three elder girls had been taken to Russia for inspection, and the Grand Duke Constantine had chosen Juliana himself (laconically remarking that she was the "least ugly"), but the marriage, on which so many hopes were placed, was unhappy from the start. As a contemporary noted, "The Grand Duchess was charming. Her husband neglected her; she consoled herself, and the conse-quences of her consolation forced her to leave Russia in 1801, never to return."[2] The divorce was concluded only in 1820, "by order of the Tsar", and at the same time Constantine renounced his claim to the imperial throne, in order to con-tract a new, morganatic marriage. Thus Juliana of Coburg lost her chance of becoming tsarina, for in 1825, on the death of Constantine's elder brother, he refused his rightful crown on the basis of his former oath of renunciation.

The Coburgs would have been shattered at their daughter's disregard of Russian splendour, for their perquisites had been by no means negligible as a consequence of the match, but for-tunately for them, imperial favour was retained through Juliana's sister Antoinette. In 1798, she had married Alexander of Württemburg, brother of the Tsarina Marie Feodorovna, and did much to make up for the misbehaviour of Juliana.

Of the two remaining ducal daughters, Sophia married a French émigré with estates in Austria, Emmanuel Mensdorff-Pouilly, and Victoire the widower Prince Emich Charles of Leiningen.

Emich Charles was born in 1763, the son of the Count of Leiningen-Dachsburg-Hadenburg, whose ancestry stretched back to 1096 but whose territory extended only some 250 metres on the left bank of the Rhine, from the Moselle in the north to the Pfalz region in the south. His father had been in the service of Frederick the Great in his wars with the French, and in 1779 had reaped his reward in advancement to the title of Prince of Leiningen. Emich Charles was less fortunate; in his father's old age, he had himself sided with his patron against the

French, but this time it was to the Leiningens' disadvantage. With the invasion of Germany by the French in 1793, the family fled, leaving their tiny capital, Durkheim, to be burned by the conquerors in January of 1794. Exile was somewhat sweetened by the granting of land around Amorbach in Lower Franconia, by the Treaty of Luneville—which also formally deprived Emich Charles's father of the possession, though not of the title, of his former estates. It was not until November 1802 that the old Prince, his sister and his son Emich Charles arrived at their new home, a miniature palace off the market-place of the village of Amorbach, in one of the deeply-wooded valleys of the Odenwald, between the rivers Main and Neckar.

The heir to this pocket-principality came as a widower, having lost his young wife, Sophia Henrietta of Lobenstein-Ebersdorff, and their seven-year-old son before the Luneville treaty was accomplished. Thus it came about that he presented his suit at Coburg, for the hand of the seventeen-year-old Victoire, and was accepted. At one time, by some (unsubstantiated) accounts, the girl might have hoped for a match which would eclipse all others: it is said that in 1802, her name was on the list of princesses offered to the conquering Napoleon, who was considering putting away Josephine in favour of a grander marriage-partner. True or not, the prospects came to nothing, and Victoire was given to one who had good cause to hate the French 'corporal'. After prolonged negotiations which led to a formidable contract of marriage (preserved at Amorbach in a red plush book, with large silver seals), the wedding of Victoire and Emich Charles took place at Coburg on 21st December 1803.

Victoire's new husband was twenty-three years her senior, a good business-man (he initiated a lumber industry at Amorbach which is still its major money-spinner), devoted to the theatre, painting and literature—and to hunting, attractive and witty, but of an "uncertain temper", embittered by his recent misfortunes. Yet, if it was no love-match, nor with the grandeur of the marriages of her elder sisters, Victoire had compensations in her new position. Her husband was pleased at the high connections his marriage had given him, and hoped for favours from his new relations; thus, whatever the charms of his wife herself, he was eager to ingratiate himself with her. They shared a love of music, and in the early days at least, would sit down together to play duets and sing.

Amorbach itself was pleasing, too, and more 'romantic' in its scenery than pasture-land Coburg. In the bride's first months in her new home, Amorbach must have looked very much as it did when the author of this book visited it in August 1972: a sleepy little village basking in summer sunshine, but occasionally threatened by the sudden, violent storms to be encountered in the Odenwald at that time of year. In the afternoon shadow of the Catholic church lies the little eighteenth-century palace, facing on to the market-place with its old *Rathaus*, and its gaily-frescoed houses stretching over the brow of the hill. Only a few hundred yards away stands the (now Protestant) abbey, with a fine prospect over the valley. Its bells ring out frequently, answered by those of the Catholic church; the abbey boasts a fine organ—of five thousand pipes, in the gallery overlooking the multi-coloured baroque and rococo decorations of the church. If Amorbach's abbey lacks the 'dim religious light' conducive to spiritual meditation, it has an airy brightness, not to say gaudiness, which could well turn the mind to the glories of a cheerful Heaven. Beyond the cloisters, across the paved square, is the entrance to the princely *Seegarten*, the park opened on Victoire's twenty-fourth birthday with sentimental festivities, now free to the public, who may wander its shady paths beside the swan-lake.

But Emich Charles and Victoire were not long to enjoy domestic peace, before fresh incursions by the French shattered Germany. Amorbach had little to tempt the invaders, though it bore its full share of plundering soldiery, but Victoire's old home, Coburg, suffered direct attacks, and the ducal palace itself came under fire. Victoire's father had become duke in 1805, and struggled vainly to meet the difficulties he was faced with; unable to find safety for his family at neighbouring Saalfeld, while the French occupied Coburg, Duke Francis returned home, frightened and ill, to negotiate the admission of his duchy to the French-inspired Confederation of the Rhine—an admission of his defeat. But he died on 9th December 1806, a few days before the treaty was signed.

For some months, the situation was perilous: the new Duke, Victoire's brother Ernest, was with the Prussian army, and was himself suffering from typhus. The courageous widowed Duchess Augusta, who had been the strength of the family ever since the days of forced economy, set off to find Napoleon, to beg his mercy on her home, but was unable to catch up with him in his swift tour of middle Europe. The Coburgs suffered the imposition of a French *intendant* to administer the duchy, until the mediation of the Tsar at Tilsit in 1807 saw young Duke Ernest restored to his lands. This was not the end of the problem, however, for now the family faced the dilemma of the Coburg forces being absorbed into the French army, with Ernest under the command of the Emperor, while his younger brother Ferdinand served with the still recalcitrant Austrians. The youngest Coburg prince, Leopold, held Russian army offices (of an honorary sort, at that time, but nevertheless distasteful to the French Emperor) and might at any time be called to follow French colours.

At Amorbach, Victoire, like her mother in Coburg, had to cope with the domestic disturbances caused by military occupation, and had also to bear with her husband's passions at his inability to protect his people. He may well have blamed his wife's family that he did not share in the protection they enjoyed; he was utterly disappointed in the hopes he had cherished when he married Victoire. In 1808, he wrote bitterly of the Coburgs to Duke Ernest's mistress: "I cannot sufficiently recommend you to distrust them. For have I not myself been the dupe of their promises? And did they not assure me with fair words before I entered their family? And since I entered it, they have not kept a single one of their engagements."[3] Nevertheless, Victoire herself did her duty by the Prince of Leiningen: she gave him two fine children. The elder was Charles Frederick William (named after his grandfather, the first Prince, who died in 1807), who was born on 12th September 1804; the younger was born on 7th December 1807, a girl named

Anna Feodorovna (for her aunt Juliana who had adopted the saint's name and Russian patronimic at the time of her marriage), though known in the family as Feodora or Feodore.

But amid the sudden alarums of war, there were periods of peace, and when the roads were considered safe, the Dowager Duchess Augusta could visit her daughter. Despite the privations of war, a splendid entertainment was arranged for Augusta, and for the Grand Duchess Constantine who accompanied her to Amorbach, on New Year's Day 1808. The Leiningens gave a ball, at which all the guests were attired in Russian costume, in honour of Juliana. The three-year-old Charles "appeared as a Cossack with a bow and arrow, looking quite like a little Cupid, whose weapons he carried",[4] wrote the Dowager Duchess in her journal. She also recorded her admiration of the happy family life which her youngest daughter had created despite such trying circumstances. A year later, Augusta described her grandson as "a dear clever boy, full of life and go", while Feodora was "a sweet little pickle, who already now, shows grace in every movement of her small body".[5]

At Coburg, on return visits, Victoire found many sad changes. Since the sudden invasions of 1806, the duchy had known little respite from visitations of predatory troops; the peasantry was impoverished and the usually fruitful land largely uncultivated. Of the 250 Coburg men who were swept off to fight in Spain, only eighteen returned, and in January 1813, the newly-replenished force was almost annihilated at Vilna in the north.

When peace came, Duchess Augusta was at Amorbach once more, and thus, in her invaluable diary, gives us a picture of the reaction to the receipt of the news that Paris had fallen. It arrived on Good Friday 1814:

With an enthusiasm that can never be equalled we heard the news of this great event. Leiningen ordered the church bells to be rung immediately and their beautiful deep tones sounded impressively in the calm night. One could hear from the Roman Catholic church the soft sounds of Good Friday's closing service, and their bells also started to ring as soon as this ended.

An unheard-of thing on Good Friday! The air reverberated with cheers from the populace and the constant firing of guns, which echoed in the hills.[6]

Three months after the peace, Augusta had less momentous but more personal news to record: Emich Charles, Prince of Leiningen, had died on 4th July. He had been ill for some time but, just when his doctors had thought that he was improving, pneumonia supervened, and he was too weak to fight it. Augusta sincerely regretted the loss of her son-in-law:

His many good qualities were somewhat spoilt by his hasty temper and obstinacy which made him enemies. . . . The last years of Leiningen's life had been a constant struggle between inimical feelings and a restless striving to get back his independence—a thing impossible to obtain any more. When I went to Amorbach last winter I found him much altered and his spirit broken. He was more mild and friendly than I had seen him for years, but he seemed very weary both in mind and body. Seldom did his sparkling spontaneity of former years break out, which had made intercourse with him so attractive. He did, however, occasionally let fall some caustic remark about the world's events. I was convinced he would not have to endure life much longer, though I little thought his end was so near. I shall always treasure pleasant memories of his friendliness during the last months of his life.[7]

Whatever memories Victoire may have had of her husband, his death must have come as a shock: she was only twenty-seven, and burdened with two young children. Her mother remarked that Leiningen's death was, to his widow, "naturally a great grief, but not a calamity"[8]—a sad epitaph both to the man and to the marriage, but perhaps reasonable in view of the circumstances of the match, and the trials of the war years which so strained the relationship. Many a husband's death was greeted with perfect composure, occasionally joy, by the victims of aristocratic arranged marriages.

But if Victoire had grief and regrets, in the first days of her widowhood, she had the comforting company of her sister Sophia and her brothers Ernest and Ferdinand. However, she was not able to stay in conventional retirement for long, even had she been the most sorrowing of wives, for her son, the new Prince of Leiningen, was only nine years old, and a regency on his behalf was inevitable. Victoire might well view with trepidation the probability of imposition of rule from Bavaria or Baden, whose respective King and Duke were the executors of her late husband. It is, however, some indication (rare enough in the sparse annals of Victoire's life at this period) of her capabilities and strength of mind, that it was to Victoire rather than to an outsider that the regency was awarded. The task was no sinecure in those difficult post-war years in Germany, with the depletion of the essential manpower in that agricultural region, and amid the poverty of peasantry, *bourgeoisie* and aristocracy alike after more than a decade of upheaval.

One member of the family unable to visit Victoire after her bereavement was her brother Leopold, the Coburgs' Benjamin whom all had feared would be drafted into the French army. The closest the Prince got, however, to the French eagles, was in the salons of the galaxy of beauties of Napoleon's court, on a trip to Paris with his eldest brother: he had quite enchanted the Bonaparte ladies, it was reported to his disapproving mother. But the family's natural allegiance was with the Russians, and in 1814 Leopold had ridden into Paris in the train of the triumphant Allies, as a member of the Tsar's entourage. When the glittering assembly moved on to England to be fêted there by the Prince Regent, Leopold followed— though he had doubts as to whether he could afford the expenses of such a pleasure trip. June 1814 was to find him lodged over a shop in a London back-street, but enjoying the company of the highest of the land in mansions and palaces.

One of Leopold's new acquaintances was the Princess Charlotte, the daughter of the Prince Regent and hence second in line to the throne of England. Though engaged to the Prince of Orange at the time, Charlotte was attracted to the dark good looks of the young Coburg. After discarding her fiancé, whom she had always despised, and having lost the Prussian prince whom she admired, the Princess came, a year or so later, seriously to consider Leopold as a potential husband.

23

Meanwhile, he had left England, had enjoyed more festivities attendant on the first phase of the Congress of Vienna (at which Coburg was recognized as a sovereign state within the German Confederation) and had narrowly missed taking part in the Battle of Waterloo—he and his Russian brigade arrived at Brussels too late to join the encounter. In January 1816, Leopold was in Berlin when he received an invitation to go back to England, with a covering letter from the Prime Minister, Lord Castlereagh, indicating that the Prince Regent was willing that he, Leopold, should marry Princess Charlotte. Leopold arrived in England on 19th February; the wooing was brief and to the point; on 10th March, the Regent gave his consent to the marriage; on 2nd May there was a royal wedding. The youngest son of a minor German duke, like a prince in a fairy-tale, had won the greatest heiress in Europe.

The prospects were dazzling: within a few years, Leopold might well be the consort of the Queen Regnant of England—perhaps she might have him created King! If the future was awesome, however, the present was pleasant enough. Charlotte had had a difficult girlhood, and had never had anyone whom she could wholeheartedly love. Now, she adored her handsome husband. In many ways, though, she was difficult to live with, and it needed all Leopold's tact to temper her impatience and restlessness. He met the challenge with the strength of mind which was to characterize the rest of his life in many changing circumstances: "Charlotte's noble and impetuous nature", wrote her mother-in-law, "had learnt to rely on Leopold's wise and cautious counsel and his unusually cool judgment."[9]

The idyll was short-lived. At 9 pm on 5th November 1817, Charlotte was delivered of a stillborn son after some fifty hours of agonized labour. She died in the early hours of the next day.

The marriage and widowing of Prince Leopold would seem on the surface to be irrelevant to the life of his sister Victoire, far away in Amorbach, but they were, in fact, to be a turning-point.

In the troubles of Princess Charlotte's girlhood, she had gone frequently for advice to her uncle Edward, the Duke of Kent. With her happy marriage to Leopold, she sought to strengthen family ties by a match between Edward and the widowed Victoire of Leiningen. Though the Duke of Kent was at that time personally disinclined to marriage (living in perfectly satisfactory domesticity with his mistress), his financial situation was so straitened that the Parliamentary grant consequent upon a royal marriage seemed to be an answer to prayer. Accordingly, while on a visit to Germany in the autumn of 1816, he made a brief stop at Amorbach, ostensibly to deliver letters from Leopold, and took a good look at Victoire. Soon, a proposal was made.

Victoire hesitated for some time. She was worried that a second marriage, and one which would inevitably involve residence away from Amorbach, might endanger her regency for her son, which still had some years to run. And there were many minor inducements to remain in her home of fourteen years, beyond those officially represented: it was very pleasant to have control over one's own house and income (a situation unusual for any woman but a widow in that man-dominated era); it was enjoyable to be the arbiter of the petty disputes and problems of her lands; she had her friends, especially one *Seelschwester*, Polyxene von Tubeuf, and her circle of artistic and musical co-enthusiasts. Should she give up her independence, her home and her associations for the sake of an unromantic middle-aged man, albeit a royal duke, in a far-off, unknown country, whose language she could not speak? She had endured one husband many years her senior, should she—this time, of her own mature volition—accept another? Victoire of Leiningen refused the Duke of Kent's proposal.

But Charlotte and Leopold would not give up hope. Letters from her brother urged Victoire to reconsider her decision. Perhaps he made the inducements more attractive, for she hesitated, read more blandishments, then retracted her definite refusal. Given time, and more favourable circumstances, she thought that she might say 'yes'. Leopold wrote to their sister Sophia that he was very pleased with Victoire, "everything she

said to me in her last letter was most reasonable. I fear, however, that no marriage will take place this year [1817] . . . but
in an affair of this sort a move at the wrong time would ruin
everything."[10]

That ruin nearly came about. In October, the Duke of Kent
heard that his intentions were becoming common knowledge—
something which, for his own reasons, he had wished to avoid
before the matter was certain. He urged Leopold that, as soon
as Charlotte had had her baby, the matter should be finalized
one way or the other. But Charlotte's death and the subsequent
seclusion of her widower interrupted the proxy wooing.

However, the new factor of the need to provide heirs to the
throne of England to replace Charlotte, jealousy at the haste
his brothers were making to marry and beget children, and
Edward's discovery that his steps for financial retrenchment
were not as effective as they should have been, caused the
Duke of Kent to be direct with Victoire, without the mediation
of her formerly-obliging brother Leopold. On 10th January
1818, he wrote to her, asking for a "positive" answer.

Only now, after a year or more of doubt, could Victoire's
mother write in her diary: "Letters from the Duke of Kent
to Victoire and Ernest make quite clear his intention of asking
for her hand. In October 1816 and last year she could not make
up her mind, but now she is much inclined to accept and looks
forward calmly to her new life."[11] On 25th January, Victoire
wrote to Edward, accepting his proposal.

NOTES TO CHAPTER ONE

1 Bauer, *Caroline Bauer and the Coburgs*, p. 21.
2 Lieven, *Unpublished diary. . .* , p. 23.
3 Emich Charles, Prince of Leiningen to Pauline Panam, 1808:
   Bauer, *op. cit.*, p. 108.
4 Augusta, Dowager Duchess of Saxe-Coburg-Saalfeld, *In Napoleonic Days*, p. 19: 1.1.08.
5 *Ibid.*, p. 59, 20.3.09.
6 *Ibid.*, pp. 129–30: 8.4.14.
7 *Ibid.*, pp. 141–2: 5.7.14.

8 *Ibid.*
9 *Ibid.*, p. 186: 22.11.17.
10 Prince Leopold of Saxe-Coburg-Saalfeld to Sophia, Countess Mensdorff-Pouilly, 1817: Lancaster, "Tragedy at Claremont", *Cornhill Magazine*, 1937, pp. 54–5.
11 Augusta, Dowager Duchess of Saxe-Coburg-Saalfeld, *op. cit.*, p. 190: 21.1.18.

CHAPTER TWO

The Duke of Kent

At the death of the Princess Charlotte in 1817, the members of the royal family of England were aged between forty and eighty—her grandparents, King George III and Queen Charlotte, and their twelve surviving children. With the death of Charlotte, the one eligible grandchild of George III, the crown of England threatened to pass through a series of elderly royal brothers, then to their sisters, then to cousins (the Gloucesters) also childless—then whence? To the young Duke of Brunswick, the son of the old King's sister? Was the House of Hanover to be succeeded on the English throne by the House of Brunswick? Would the nation accept the imposition of a new set of foreigners as their monarchs, with their attendant entourage of money-grubbing, office-sharing parasites—would they, in fact, be willing to return to the first days of George I? To those members of the royal family with sense enough to understand the situation, it appeared that at all costs the future heir to the kingdoms must be of their own line. The horrors of the French Revolution had shown only too clearly how a whole royal dynasty might be swept away. Should the future hold no continuance of the established royal line, the monarchy might be abolished in England, too, rather than see it vested in more mistrusted, detested aliens.

How had this parlous state of affairs arisen? The answer lies in the personal lives of George III's children: while the old King had done his duty in giving the nation a large number of heirs of his body, those heirs were neither so dutiful, nor so prolific. The first was George, Charlotte's father, and since 1811 Regent of England. Already middle-aged when he took up the reins of government on the final imprisonment of his father due to 'insanity', George had waited long to taste the sweets of executive power, though he had dabbled in Opposition politics for many years. In his twenties he had formed a liaison (debatably a legal marriage) with one Maria Fitzherbert, which had proved childless; in 1795, to obtain a grant to pay his debts, he had married his cousin Caroline of Brunswick and within a year gave England an heir in the second generation—Princess Charlotte. But no brothers or sisters followed, for, according to trustworthy authorities, after assuring himself of his wife's first pregnancy, George never again shared Caroline's bed. The Princess requited her husband's loathing, took only a desultory interest in her daughter and later retired to the Continent, there to provide European newspapers with a seemingly endless supply of copy of never-failing interest and—at a time of almost universal coarseness—extreme indelicacy.

Charlotte was brought up in a family of scapegrace uncles and ageing, discontented spinster aunts. Her contact with her mother was carefully limited—fortunately for her morals—and the one period at which she did enjoy frequent meetings with Caroline produced an involvement with a Captain Hesse at which her mother certainly connived, and which luckily stopped short of 'ruining her character'. It is not surprising that Charlotte became wilful and unmanageable, antipathetic to her father and glad to gain some degree of freedom in marriage at the age of twenty. Her life promised to assure the continuation of the royal succession: at her death, one has to look back to her uncles and aunts for heirs to the throne.

Charlotte's eldest uncle was Frederick, Duke of York, married since 1791 to the barren Frederica of Prussia. Frederick still lived under the cloud of a scandal in which his mistress—and, by association, himself—was involved in the sale of army offices, after which he found it necessary to resign his post of Commander-in-Chief. While the Duke went his own way, the Duchess of York filled her days with caring for a menagerie of animals, which filled every room of her house, troubling her husband but little.

William, Duke of Clarence, was of a different type from his elder brothers. He had spent his life in naval service, more to his own amusement than to the nation's benefit. For twenty years he had lived with an actress, Dorothea Jordan, who between theatre engagements (her salary was said to line William's pockets) bore him ten children. These were the Fitzclarences, each named after a royal uncle or aunt. William's decision to beget a legitimate heir after his niece's death was followed by a feverish, and at times ludicrous, search for a wife, which ended in 1818 with the acquiescence of Adelaide of Saxe-Meiningen—of an equal age with William's eldest daughter.

Passing over Edward, Duke of Kent, who must have longer attention than his brothers, the next son of George III was Ernest, Duke of Cumberland, a man of sinister reputation and hideous appearance. His wife (whom he married in 1815) was Frederica of Mecklenburg-Strelitz, the niece of his own mother, Queen Charlotte, who, however, refused to receive her, on the grounds of former marital misconduct. Frederica had been in the process of divorcing her first husband (with her second already in view), when he unexpectedly, and rather too conveniently, died. Ernest himself was under a good deal of suspicion for the murder of his valet.

Augustus, Duke of Sussex, was innocuous by contrast. His marriage of 1793 to Lady Augusta Murray had been declared null (under the terms of the Royal Marriage Act of 1772) and their two children lived only on the periphery of the royal circle, with no rights of inheritance. Adolphus, Duke of Cambridge, was Viceroy of Hanover—and rejoiced in being the only one of the royal dukes in financial solvency. Like his brothers William and Edward, at the beginning of 1818 he entered the race for an heir, marrying Augusta of Hesse-Cassel.

The five surviving daughters of George III were Charlotte (the Princess Royal), Augusta, Elizabeth, Mary and Sophia. The youngest daughter, Amelia, had died in 1810, her demise being a contributing factor to her father's final breakdown. At the time of their niece Charlotte's death, only two of the sisterhood were married: the Princess Royal to the King of Württemburg, Mary to her cousin William, Duke of Gloucester. Both marriages proved childless. The three remaining sisters were unmarried, though Sophia was mother of a son by an army officer formerly attached to the Court. Only Elizabeth would go to the altar in the years of her middle age. She married Frederick Landgrave of Hesse-Homburg in 1818 and suffered the name 'Betty Humbug' bestowed on her by the popular Press.

In this large, interesting, unconventional family, Edward, Duke of Kent, was neither the best nor the worst. Though he had neither the obesity of the Regent nor the ugliness of Cumberland, in middle age he was by no means an Adonis; neither violent nor devious, unlike his elder brothers, he was nevertheless a hard man, often hypocritical. If his friends were unswervingly loyal, those who regarded themselves as his enemies were so more from contempt than from fear. Edward had lived away from England for most of his young manhood, and had avoided the embroilment of his brothers in domestic politics, though he was known to favour reformers and Whigs. Had he followed his brother William to the throne in 1837, Edward would have made a conscientious but not an inspiring monarch.

Edward was born on 2nd November 1767 at Buckingham House, in West London, then known more familiarly as 'The Queen's House', now (with much addition to its building) Buckingham Palace. First educated at home by tutors, in 1785 he was sent to Luneburg for military training and then on to Geneva to complete his studies. When he returned home in 1790 he was already deeply in debt, and left behind a baby daughter by a recently-dead French girl. (So far, at least, did he follow the propensities of his eldest brother.) His reception by the King was, not unreasonably, cool, and he was swiftly hustled on to a ship bound for Gibraltar where he was to begin military service with the Royal Fusiliers, of which regiment he was a colonel. He took up his duties in the Rock's garrison on equal terms with his fellow-officers, living in rough quarters such as he had never known, and feeling, on the evidence of his letters home, unbearably lonely. This latter problem was easily resolved. In January 1791 he wrote to his brother William:

> I feel the want of resources perhaps less than any man, for I manage with the assistance of a little music, a few books, and a little small talk with four or five officers, who constantly live in my family, to fill up as cheerfully as I can those moments when professional business does not occupy me. Besides I have at present a young woman living with me who I wrote over to, to come from France to me, who has every qualification which an excellent share of good temper, no small degree of cleverness, and above all, a pretty face and a handsome person can give to make my hours pass away pleasantly in her company.[1]

This woman was to be Edward's devoted companion for more than a quarter of a century: Alphonsine Thérèse Bernadine Julie de Montgenet, a *bourgeoise* from Besançon, procured for the Prince by a M. Fontiny and known to history as Julie St Laurent. Despite the remonstrations of his superiors (and attempts on their part to pay the lady off), Edward kept Julie with him, and when the regiment sailed for Canada in June 1791, 'Madame St Laurent' accompanied him.

The popularity and entertainment that the Prince enjoyed in Quebec, spiced by his light duties in the regiment, was marred in the winter of 1792–3 by an attempted mutiny, and in the subsequent courts martial Edward showed himself in a poor light through his severity in dealing with the culprits. Then, in April 1793, news arrived of France's declaration of war on England: Edward was eager for a taste of fighting, but it was not until Christmas Eve of that year that he received his orders to proceed to the West Indies, where there was some action. After a much-publicized progress through the United States, via New York to Boston (whose newspapers greeted the Prince as 'Edward Guelph' with true republican spirit), he took ship for Martinique. At last he saw the British army go into action. On the island of St Lucia, his own division took Porte Fortunée, which he renamed Port Charlotte as a compliment to his mother.

Returned to Canada, Edward was disappointed at his failure to gain either promotion or removal to further active service.

But there were compensations: in Halifax, Nova Scotia 'Madame' was more easily accepted into 'society' than she had been in Quebec, the citadel of Canadian aristocracy. In 1798, the couple left for England—Edward had had a fall from his horse and felt in need of the Bath cure, and, besides, he might be able to further his cause if he were able to apply directly to his brother the Duke of York for his career advancement. This time, his welcome home was warmer; even his critical mother was pleased to see him, noting the 'improvement' in his character—though averring the pious hope that he would maintain it while in England. He did; Julie was kept discreetly in the background, and the Duke made every effort to avoid being seen with her in public. In this he was not entirely successful, and the Duke of York (who himself admitted that he should be the last person to preach to his brother) felt it incumbent on him to warn Edward that he was not in Canada now! He was in England, where every movement of the members of the royal family was watched with fascination, and recorded in the Press. With some asperity, and at some length, Edward penned a reply to his elder brother: he had done his best to keep Julie out of sight; he understood the need for discretion; should he gain a new posting abroad, he would take care that his personal and domestic arrangements would embarrass neither his family nor his associates. The hint was not taken. There was no new posting, no promotion. The only gains with which Edward left England on his return to Canada were the dukedoms of Kent and Strathearn, bestowed upon him by his father in April 1799 (at the same time as Prince Ernest became Duke of Cumberland).

Another year in Canada, and a period of inactivity at home, only sharpened Edward's desire for a higher command. The war in Europe dragged on, until the autumn of 1801, when negotiations were opened which were to lead to the signing of the Treaty of Amiens in 1802.

Now was Edward's moment. On 27th April 1802, he embarked for Gibraltar as the appointed governor of the Rock colony.

But he had not been long in Gibraltar before he realized that all was not well with the British garrison. The basic factor in the trouble was the scarcity of water in contrast to the plenitude of wine: drunkenness—not occasional but habitual—was rife among officers and men alike. In addition, the officers were inexperienced, and, under lax supervision, had allowed discipline to deteriorate. In his eagerness to amend the situation, Edward acted quickly and somewhat over-zealously. He found it necessary to drill the ranks himself, to show his subordinates how it *should* be done, inevitably alienating them. In an attempt to curb the drinking, he closed more than half of the Rock's numerous taverns (to the detriment of his own income from the sale of licences), put out of bounds to his soldiers all but three of those remaining and opened a canteen for the sale of beer and cider as well as of the heady Spanish vintages.

The Duke of Kent was just beginning to feel satisfied that the new regime of long working-hours (to obviate the temptations of leisure) and strict observance of army regulations had produced some good effect when, at the end of December, a mutiny broke out. On Christmas Eve, at about seven in the evening, the 1st Regiment of Foot broke out of their barracks and stood, with their guns loaded and bayonets fixed, outside the Duke's house, demanding that he leave the garrison immediately, and threatening and abusing him. Other regiments were mustered, and interposed their bodies and two cannons between the mutineers and the Duke's house, eventually forcing them to return to their barracks, with promises of redress of grievances. However, some hundred and fifty of the men made for the barracks of the 54th Regiment hoping to incite them to mutiny, too, but failed as the grenadiers opened fire and wounded five of their number. The next day discontent was rife, but nothing more happened until the 26th, when the 25th Regiment marched on Edward's house, to find artillery waiting for them: two mutineers were killed (and one of their adversaries) and six wounded. Despite the knowledge that pretty well all his men had become disaffected during the last few days, Edward had fourteen men put on trial before a court martial.

Though he was determined to restore order in the garrison as soon as possible, Edward wrote home to his brother Frederick, Duke of York, the Commander-in-Chief, requesting leave of absence to begin as soon as the Rock was again quiet. It was March before the letter reached England, but before the month was out, Edward had received his brother's reply, ordering him home immediately to account for his conduct. The court martial had by then long since ended, and three men had faced a firing squad and many others had been flogged; routine duty on the Rock had been restored.

The Duke of Kent reached England on 27th May to find himself the centre of a storm of vilification. Despite the fact that several Englishmen at Gibraltar had reported the mitigating circumstances of his severity, he found that he was being accused of unwarranted cruelty and even of provocation of the mutiny. Scorning Edward's repeated expressions of his willingness to return to Gibraltar, the Duke of York refused to contemplate any further active service for his brother. For an indefinite period, he must remain at home in enforced idleness. For all that Edward had good reason to harbour resentment against Frederick of York, his loyalty overcame his bitterness when, in 1809, the latter and his mistress, Mary Anne Clarke, were involved in a scandal over their alleged sale of army appointments and promotions, and York's misuse of army funds. In 1810, however, it was Edward's turn to endure calumny—in the vituperation of Mrs Clarke published in her book *The Rival Princes*, in which she claimed that Edward had engineered the Gibraltar mutiny to oust his brother (who would take the ultimate responsibility) from his post as Commander-in-Chief, in order to gain the honour himself. It was to be many years before harmony was restored in the royal family, whose members took sides in the dispute with great zest.

Edward's history in the years after his retirement from the Army until 1816 is mainly the history of his family and nation. His sister Amelia died in 1810, and the King finally lapsed into darkness in a padded cell at Windsor; George, Prince of Wales, became Regent, and his wife, Princess Caroline, continued to shock the nation with her misdemeanours. Trafalgar was fought and won, and Nelson died; Napoleon marched through Europe and threatened the shores of Britain; then came the Russian fiasco and the long march home, the Allied attack on France, Napoleon's exile to Elba—his return and Waterloo. And throughout these stirring events, Edward was only an observer, an avid consumer of newspapers. Failing to win a more active role in his country's affairs, he took up 'good works' instead.

Could he now settle into comfortable middle age, secure in Julie's affections, free of the demands of his rank, sympathetic with his family—with an untroubled horizon? Unfortunately, he could not. The Duke of Kent's debts had been mounting up over the past quarter of a century. On the surface, his income seemed more than adequate: in 1799 he had enjoyed an annual grant of £10,900; a further £12,000 per annum had been voted from the Civil List in 1802; when he gained the Gibraltar governorship, his gross income stood at £19,417 a year; in October 1805, Edward, like his brothers, had a windfall of £20,000 from the Admiralty droits. From 1806 he could rely on a definite £18,000 a year. The fluctuations were caused mainly by the enjoyment or otherwise of the perquisites of his offices, and by the varying rents of his estates, as well as by the different standards of living required by service abroad or residence in England.

But at the end of 1806, Edward finally faced a reckoning of his debts which horrified him. The total sum demanded by his creditors was £108,200. For ten years, Edward tried various means of liquidating the debt, but unforeseen accidents, such as the failure of his bankers in 1810 and the absconding of his solictor in 1814, hampered his efforts. When Edward poured out his woes to those who might have helped him—his family —he never failed to remind them that he had lost some £36,450 worth of equipment and possessions in the service of his country, when, on four occasions, English ships transporting them were either seized or sunk by the French. But no one would help him out of his difficulties. When Edward realized that his future freedom from pestering creditors depended entirely on his own efforts, he arranged that £17,000 of his current annual £25,000 should go towards paying it off, and computed that if he could manage on the remainder, incurring no more debts, all should be settled by the year 1821. Accordingly, early in March 1816, the Duke of Kent made a brief trip to Brussels to look for a house to be rented cheaply.

Then, during the summer, an alternative expedient suggested itself. In May of that year, Princess Charlotte, Edward's niece, married Leopold of Saxe-Coburg-Saalfeld, and the newly-weds suggested to Edward that his own marriage (or rather, the financial grant from Parliament which he would receive on its accomplishment) would be a swifter means than retrenchment of rectifying his pecuniary embarrassment. Charlotte and Leopold mooted an alliance for Edward with Leopold's sister Victoire, the widowed Princess of Leiningen, but the Princess Catherine of Baden was also a feasible candidate. As sister of the Tsarina of Russia, she would be a good connexion, thought Edward—and the Tsar obviously agreed, for he lent the Duke the wherewithal to visit his sister-in-law Catherine.

Thus, in the months before Edward and Julie took up residence in Brussels, he made a round tour of Germany, with the ostensible reason of visiting his eldest sister, the Queen of Württemburg, but taking in Baden to see the Princess. She was over forty and very plain. Duly, Edward proceeded to Amorbach, to take a look at the Princess Victoire. There, he saw nothing to make him averse to the idea of marrying her— saving always the disagreeable business of parting from Julie after so many years. (Unlike his brothers, Edward was too conscientious—or too conventional—to contemplate retaining his mistress after he had acquired a wife.) Throughout the winter of 1816–17, negotiations went on between Edward and Victoire —not the hesitations of a romantic attachment, but the practicalities of a match which would be arranged to their mutual advantage. Victoire was worried that she might lose the guardianship of her son. Accordingly, she refused the Duke's offer— then, under pressure from the Coburg family, temporized.

If Victoire was uncertain what to do for the best, Edward was even more indecisive. He was anxious to keep the whole thing a secret, not only for fear of hurting Julie, but so as not to apprise his brother the Regent, who might force the issue, while there was still a chance of averting the whole break-up of Edward's domestic bliss. But the carelessness of the Duke's lawyers, then engaged in the negotiations, alerted the Press to the situation. On 6th February 1817, a notice appeared in the London *Morning Chronicle*, which was partially reprinted in a Continental paper, stating baldly that Edward was to marry Victoire of Leiningen. This leak of his intentions threw Edward into a panic. Writing to one of his friends, Frederick Wetherall, he described Julie's reaction on seeing the announcement: it "produced *no* heat or violence on *her* part, but a scene more truly distressing or heartbreaking than *any* I ever yet went thro', yet the whole of which does equal honor to her head and to her heart . . . it has made a very deep impression on her, the subject is frequently reverted to and occasions infinitely uncomfortable moments to both".[2] Edward asked his friend that when next he wrote to him, he should insert in the letter a paragraph (which Edward himself drafted) to the effect that he, Wetherall, had heard the rumours of the marriage and had denied them publicly, knowing Edward's devotion to 'Madame'. The Duke added that there were so many difficulties in the way of the match – not only on Victoire's side, but in his duty to leave Julie comfortably provided for, and in the least possible distress, that it might never come to anything at all.

Though Edward was spared further embarrassment in the international Press during the summer, on 7th November 1817, the *Morning Chronicle* revived its rumours. In view of the recent death of Princess Charlotte,

It will be the earnest prayer of the nation, that an early alliance of one of the unmarried Princes may forthwith be settled. There were some time ago rumours of the intended marriage of the truly amiable and excellent Duke of Kent, with a Princess of the House of Saxe-Coburg, one of the sisters of Prince Leopold, and we have reason to believe there was foundation for the report. Their [*sic*] is no union which the nation would hail with more rapturous delight, and for the establishment of which they would be more prompt liberally to contribute. We trust that this melancholy and unlooked-for event [the death of Charlotte] will accelerate the auspicious alliance, which may yet secure the inheritance of the crown to the lineal descendants of his majesty till the latest posterity. . . .[3]

This time, the news had a horrifying effect on Julie. Edward had read that edition of the *Morning Chronicle* over breakfast one morning, but had failed to notice the offending article. Then he tossed the paper across the table to his mistress. Suddenly, he heard "an extraordinary noise and a strong convulsive movement in Madame St Laurent's throat".[4] She had seen the paragraph, and had taken in its import.

Through an intermediary in England, the editor responsible was put on his honour to maintain silence on the subject; proprietors of foreign papers were similarly advised. At all costs, Edward would protect Julie from the misery of his loss until that loss became absolutely certain. He still hoped that the Regent might divorce and remarry, or that the Duke of Clarence would find a wife and gain for him a release from the duty himself. But talk of the royal weddings was in the air; Edward's plans could be kept secret from Julie, but not from his family. For England, the death of the Princess Charlotte had turned Edward's bid to marry for money into a patriotic gesture towards securing the royal succession in a new generation; for the royal family, it had become a race between the brothers as to who should marry first, and who should beget the heir.

On 10th January 1818, unable to bear the suspense any longer, Edward wrote to Victoire of Leiningen asking for a definite answer to his proposal. He received her reply—an acceptance—within the month.

Edward could not face up to the upheaval in his life that was now coming. He clung to the hope that his elder brother William, the Duke of Clarence, might marry and that he might still be freed from having to do so himself, by some dynastic and financial miracle. But, even though there was no news of the confirmation of Victoire's regency, Edward prepared to go to England in March, to make arrangements for his marriage, and did his best to hide from Julie the real reason for his going. He again asked Wetherall to write him a letter which might be "shewable" to Julie, in which he was to request the Duke to return home on urgent business. Thus, he might leave Madame St Laurent behind without her suspecting that she might never see him again. Daily he was suffering from her unhappiness, for "tho' she behaves *admirably* about it I see her *tears floating down her Cheeks*, and, at *times*, notwithstanding all her Endeavour to struggle and bear up, she lets out her fears, alarms, and suspicions."[5]

But no news came from England on either the Regent's divorce or the Duke of Clarence's marriage; neither was there yet any word from Germany on the disposal of the Leiningen regency. The weather was cold and damp, and both Edward and Julie took chills. Though his departure was scheduled for 14th March, his ill-health and natural unhappiness at making the final break caused Edward to delay in Brussels until the 19th. There is no record of the parting—on Edward's side with almost certain knowledge that he would never see Julie again, on hers only suspicions that this might be the case. Their ways parted : he to England, she to Paris.

On 24th March, *The Times* announced the Duke of Kent's arrival in England. He found his family much as he expected— his father a prisoner at Windsor, his mother cheerfully ailing, the Regent fulminating against his wife, Clarence and Cambridge preparing to marry. Sometime before April, when Parliament began to debate the royal brothers' new allowances, and when the Duke's intentions were made public (since his bride's continuance as Leiningen Regent had been confirmed), he must have written to Julie of his plans, to spare her reading the tidings from the newspapers unprepared. If Julie wept at the prospect of losing Edward in his marriage, many men in England were groaning at the expense of the match. There was a good deal of prejudice, both in Parliament and throughout the nation, to the proposed increases in princely grants. The Duke of Wellington was later to exclaim, on the subject of the royal dukes: "They are the damnedest millstones about the necks of any Government that can be imagined. They have insulted—*personally* insulted—two-thirds of the gentlemen of England, and how can it be wondered at that they take their revenge upon them when they can get them in the House of Commons? It is their only opportunity, and I think, by God! they are quite right to use it."[6]

Lord Castlereagh put the royal case to Parliament: the £6,000 they were being asked to find for Edward would, he said, scarcely compensate the bride for the income and independence she was giving up:

He must say, in justice to this illustrious lady, and it was a feature of her conduct highly creditable to her, and which, he was sure, would recommend her to the respect of the Committee, that although, when the treaty of marriage was in progress, she felt it her duty not to relinquish the personal guardianship of her children, by her former marriage, she did not extend that disposition to the pecuniary advantages of her widowhood; but that her marriage would deprive her of an income of £3,000 a year on that score, and of other smaller pecuniary advantages arising from her guardianship, amounting, in the whole, to about £5,000 a year; so that the provision of a dower for her, in the event of her surviving her illustrious husband, was but an act of bare justice.[7]

On 15th May the final formalities were set in train: on a division, Edward's additional grant of £6,000 a year was carried by 205 to 52. The resolution for a dower was also passed.

The next day, Edward set off for Germany and his wedding.

NOTES TO CHAPTER TWO

1 Prince Edward to Prince William, January 1791: RA 46669: Gillen. *The Prince and his Lady*, p. 21.
2 Edward, Duke of Kent to General Wetherall, 11.2.17: RA Add 7/1246: Gillen, *op. cit.*, p. 214.
3 *Morning Chronicle*, 7.11.17.
4 Maxwell (ed.), *Creevey Papers*, volume i, p. 269: 11.12.17.
5 Edward, Duke of Kent, to General Wetherall, 23.2.18: RA Add 7/1301: Gillen, *op. cit.*, p. 223.
6 Maxwell (ed.), *op. cit.*, volume i, p. 277: 17.7.18.
7 Neale, *Life of H.R.H. Edward, Duke of Kent*, pp. 390–1.

CHAPTER THREE

A Marriage of Convenience

On 25th May, Victoire of Leiningen arrived at her mother's dower-house at Ketschendorff, just outside the town of Coburg, to spend with her the last days before her wedding. On the 26th, the family was dining when a courier arrived with the news that the Duke of Kent was to be expected within two hours—a whole day early. "We waited with much curiosity," wrote the Dowager Duchess in her diary, "and poor Victoire with a beating heart"[1]—understandable trepidation as she had seen her prospective bridegroom only once before, and that over a year previously. But Victoire had coped with an elderly husband before, and had survived the ordeal; at the time of her second wedding, she was a mature woman, knowledgeable in the ways of men, and confident that the Duke of Kent approached his forthcoming union with her with the best of intentions for her happiness.

Indeed, it was Edward who was the more embarrassed, when he found himself in the midst of the family, under close scrutiny, on his arrival. But he made a good impression, the Dowager Duchess later noting that "He is a fine man for his age, has a pleasant winning manner, and a good-humoured expression. His tall stature helps to give him an air of breeding, and he combines a simple soldierlike manner with the refinement of a man of the world, which makes intercourse with him easy and pleasant."[2] But scarcely two days were allowed for further acquaintance, and at 1 pm on the 28th, the Coburgs assembled at the Schloss Ehrenburg for the betrothal ceremony, at which the couple exchanged rings, and which was followed by a big dinner and a concert.

The 30th was the wedding day. At eight-thirty in the evening, Victoire and her mother drove again from Ketschendorff to the Schloss in the town. The *Riesensaal*, the great hall of the palace more familiarly known as the 'Hall of the Giants', by reason of the huge brightly-painted figures which serve as pillars, was brilliantly lit. Its long mirrors reflected the many flickering candles, playing on the colourful rococo decor, and the richly gilded plaster of the ceiling. The Duke was waiting for his bride under a velvet canopy, dressed in his Field-Marshal's uniform. Victoire wore a white dress, trimmed with white roses and orange blossom.

Beyond the palace, the townsfolk were told of the accomplishment of the ceremony by a cannonade.

Only two days were allowed for the honeymooners in Coburg, before they left to begin the arduous journey to England. Victoire's mother, who had watched the wedding with the pious hope that "the dear good child find in this second marriage all the happiness which she had not quite attained in her last one. . .",[3] now comforted herself with the thought that her daughter "will be very happy with her really very amiable husband, who only in middle age, makes acquaintance with family life and will therefore perhaps appreciate it all the more."[4]

But neither the Duke nor the new Duchess of Kent can have been so confident of future happiness as they drove away, almost strangers, to their unknown future. They must have taken stock of each other for the first time, away from the smothering concern of the Coburgs. A contemporary describes the Duke and Duchess of Kent as they were at that time:

The Duke of Kent, then fifty-one years of age, was a tall, stately man, of soldierlike bearing, already inclined to great corpulency. In spite of the entire baldness of the whole crown of his head, and his dyed hair, he might still be considered a handsome man. His dress was simple, but in good taste, and scrupulously neat and nice. . . . His manner in society was pleasant and easy, intentionally courteous and engaging, as he possessed the gift of speech in no small degree, he expressed himself in

English and French with a certain degree of eloquence and elegance. The play of his countenance betrayed calculation. He was not without ability and culture, and he possessed great activity. His dependants complained of his strictness and pedantic love of order. . . .

The widowed Princess of Leiningen . . . was of middle height, rather large, but with a good figure with fine brown eyes and hair, fresh and youthful, naturally cheerful and friendly, altogether most charming and attractive. She was fond of dress, and dressed well and in good taste. Nature had endowed her with warm feelings, and she was naturally truthful, affectionate, and friendly, unselfish, full of sympathy, and generous.[5]

Now, for the first time, Victoire was to be parted from her children: Charles had already left for Switzerland with his tutor, Georg Wagner, and Feodora had been left with her grandmother.

But if the journey from Coburg was strained or embarrassing for the Kents (and surely it was not, with his easy flow of talk, and her natural vivacity), as they approached Frankfurt, one of the many stopping-places *en route*, they were to be cheered with a loyal festivity at a town on the borders of the Leiningen estates. As *The Times* reported a fortnight later:

The Duke of Kent was the other day agreeably surprised by a reception at once pleasing and singular. On his entering the little town of Bisschosgeim [Tauberbischoffsheim] on the frontier of Leiningen, he was preceded by all the young girls, taste-fully dressed in white, decorated with ribands and garlands of roses, who strewed flowers before his carriage, and expressed their gratitude to him for his kindness and condescension in passing through their little town. The Duke conversed for some time with the principal inhabitants. . . .[6]

And so to Brussels, and on to the coast, to take ship at Calais for England.

The second wedding ceremony—necessary to satisfy England that the couple had been blessed by the nation's established Church, and to prevent doubts as to the validity of the marriage from being expressed at a later date, when they might affect the succession to the throne of the children of the union —was planned for 11th July. Edward and Victoire were to share the honours with William, Duke of Clarence, and

Adelaide of Saxe-Meiningen. The latter had arrived in London only on 4th July and had had but a week to make the acquaintance of her elderly and disreputable fiancé. But, as the event approached, Queen Charlotte proved too ill to attend, and the wedding was postponed until the 13th, when she was well enough to be present, though the service was shortened so as not to tire her.

A temporary altar was fitted up in the Queen's drawing-room at Kew, where the windows overlooked the wonderful gardens. The royal family and officers of State crowded into the room, which already contained the officiating Archbishop of Canterbury, the Bishop of London and their assistants. The two brides entered, in all their finery, to the unashamed stares of their new relations. Victoire at least, made a good showing, overshadowing the shy, plain Adelaide. The *Lady's Magazine* was to offer a description of her wedding-dress, much finer than that used in Germany:

A very rich and elegant gold tissue, with two superb borders of scalloped lama [*sic*] flouncing, each border headed with rich gold trimming; the body and sleeves to correspond, richly trimmed with Brussels point lace, and tastefully ornamented with gold tassels; the robe of rich gold tissue, lined with white satin, and trimmed round with rich scalloped lama trimming to match the dress, and fastened at the waist with a very brilliant diamond clasp. Head-dress, a wreath of diamonds.[7]

After the ceremony, at which both brides were given away by the Prince Regent, the family (all but the Queen, who could stand no more of her noisy brood), dined together at five o'clock. Then, at seven, the Kents drove away in Prince Leopold's coach to his mansion near Esher, Claremont, leaving their relations to drink their health in tea in the ornamental cottage near the Pagoda in Kew Gardens.

Once again, there was to be no honeymoon. Two days after the wedding, the royal brides were paraded before the Court at a large function (some six hundred people attended) at Carlton House. The affair was "dull and heavy",[8] according to one guest, and he did not admire the new Duchesses, noting that Adelaide was too thin, though her manners were good, and that Victoire, the better looking of the two, was rather plump. A popular periodical was easier to please—and more polite, telling its readers: "The person of her Serene Highness is tall and majestic; with plastic and expressive features; and a suavity and ease in her manners and deportment that engage all hearts."[9]

Throughout the summer, the Kents were to be seen everywhere. There was the large family to visit: the old Queen and her daughters at Kew, the royal dukes and duchesses in London —and always Leopold, to-ing and fro-ing between London and Claremont, eager to smooth his sister's path. But the new Duchess of Kent had adapted herself without problems; her husband was eager to please her with gifts and amusements, and to sweeten the duties—none of them at all rigorous, which she was called upon to perform. On 27th July, a deputation came up from the City of London, headed by the Lord Mayor, to offer 'felicitations' at Carlton House, Clarence House and Kensington Palace (where the Kents had been loaned apartments) on the recent bridals. Still in the earliest stages of acquiring English, which she found extremely difficult, the Duchess of Kent must needs reply to their kind wishes in a speech written out for her in phonetics. Hopefully, the dignitaries heard:

My Lord Mayor and Gentlemen : I have to regret being as yet so little conversant with the English language, which obliges me to say in a very few words that I am most grateful for your congratulations and good wishes, and highly flattered by your allusions to my brother. May I only be as fortunate as he in meriting your attachment.[10]

Edward was enthusiastic at his wife's readiness to be interested in his charitable concerns (of which, it has been computed, he was patron of over fifty). In the first week of August, the couple were present at a meeting of the trustees of the British and Foreign Schools Society, held at Southwark, and then went on to inspect a branch of the Society at the City Road. Here Edward replied to an address on his wife's behalf, and in her name gave a donation of £50. With the formation of a Ladies' Committee, Victoire took a seat, to become the first royal lady to serve a public charity. Other outings included a visit to the Woolwich Arsenal and factories, a tour of the Millbank Penitentiary (on the site of the modern Tate Gallery) and a walk through the Houses of Parliament.

Evening entertainments, besides family dinners and appearances at the Regent's Court, mainly comprised theatre visits. On 16th July the Kents were at Covent Garden to see *Rob Roy* and *The Miller and his Men*, arriving late, so that the performance had to be suspended while the 'customary honours' were paid them. Next day, *The Times* noted that Victoire "looked around her as if she expected to find in every face that of a friend, and seemed as much at home as if she had been born among us. . .".[11] The following evening it was the turn of the Coburg Theatre, named in honour of Leopold soon after his marriage to Princess Charlotte. In the interval a painted curtain was dropped, displaying a view of Claremont, where the popular Princess had died. It was "not lost upon the audience"[12] that Victoire wept a few tears—and it certainly did her no harm to evince an attachment to the memory of the girl that all England had mourned. The Duchess of Kent was beginning to woo the public.

But the expenses of the summer, despite the Parliamentary grant, were worrying Edward. The Kents were to winter in Germany, a potential economy, but first they were to stay in Valenciennes, Brussels and Aix to see something of the festivities consequent on the gathering of sovereigns there for the international treaty-making. To make a good showing there, Edward had to borrow a considerable sum of money on the security of his future income. On 6th September, the *Royal Sovereign* took on her passengers, and weighed anchor at 3 am on the 7th.

The towns of the Netherlands, in those autumn days of 1818, were gay and bustling, thronged with royalty and aristocrats, and not a few sharp-eyed observers of lesser rank. One such was the English diarist Creevey, who had some previous acquaintance with the Duke of Kent, and who enjoyed a few laughs at his expense with his crony the Duke of Wellington. They sniggered at Edward's appearance (". . . but for his blue ribbon and star, he might have passed for an orderly sergeant"[13]); they nudged each other when the Duke touched his wife's cheek to see that she was not over-heated after waltzing; they cackled at the memory of Wellington's refusal to lead Victoire's old German lady-in-waiting in to dinner, calling up the mayor of Valenciennes to take on the tiresome duty.

Leaving this not-altogether-congenial company behind, on 9th October Edward and Victoire began their journey south. *The Times* had announced on 28th September that the Kents were to go straight to "Amersbach on the Rhine", but first there was to be a trip, so enjoyable to the devotees of the Romantic and the 'Gothick', to the awe-inspiring mountains of Switzerland, where they visited Victoire's sister Juliana, and viewed the glaciers above Grindelwald, and went to the valley of Lauterburg to see the Staubbach.

It was only six months since Victoire had left Amorbach as Princess of Leiningen. Returning now as Duchess of Kent, she took up her duties as her son's regent with her new husband's help. Although her son was away from home, undergoing education, Victoire was welcomed by her nine-year-old daughter, who soon learned to love the amiable step-father who had always been so fond of other people's children and could now cherish one with a closer tie. He was also ready to admire the little principality, and to indulge his propensity for 'improving' property. Despite his previous intention to live with the utmost economy, Edward could not resist turning the tiny and rather dilapidated little palace into a more comfortable home. Borrowing some £10,000, he brought an army of English workmen into Amorbach, under the supervision of one Captain Hulme, and soon had the gardens walled into some semblance of privacy, new stoves put in and new stables erected. These latter, and the fine horses they were to house, were his especial pride, and Prince Metternich, who visited the Kents at that time, wrote to a friend: "The Duke regaled me incessantly with his stables, the particular pleasure which his new home affords him."[14]

But the greatest pleasure of all came from Edward's knowledge that his wife was pregnant. Already the Duchesses of

Victoire, Princess of Leiningen and later Duchess of Kent—a portrait from the Palace at Amorbach (reproduced by courtesy of the Amorbach Archives)

(*left*) Victoire, Duchess of Kent—a miniature by W. C. Ross, 1829 (reproduced by gracious permission of H.M. The Queen); (*below*) The Riesensaal in the Schloss Ehrenburg, Coburg (photo by Dorothea Hildebrand, Coburg)

Clarence and Cambridge had been pronounced to be *enceinte*, and now the Duchess of Kent (swiftly followed by the Duchess of Cumberland) was entering the stakes whose prize was the heir to the English throne. Edward was overjoyed. On New Year's Eve, he penned a note to Victoire which concluded with the words, written in English: "God bless you. Love me as I love you."[15]

The Duke of Kent had always maintained that his child should be born in England, and as 1819 opened, began to prepare for the journey home to be undertaken in the spring. In this project, Edward showed foresight and a shrewd summation of the feeling in England: he was well aware of the nation's wish to forget the German origins of its ruling dynasty, and he realized that England would be more likely to welcome an heir who had the minimum of foreign connections. As he wrote to a friend on 19th March, "The interesting situation of the Duchess causes me hourly anxiety; and you, who so well know my views and feelings can well appreciate how eagerly desirous I am to hasten our departure for Old England. *The event* is thought likely to occur about the end of next month. My wish is, that it may take place on the 4th of June, as that is the birth-day of my revered father; and that the child, too, like him, may be BRITON-BORN."[16]

But Edward's plan of bringing home his wife for the confinement did not have the approval of the Prince Regent. When Edward applied to him for the loan of a royal yacht for the Channel crossing, he was met with a blank refusal. Let the Duchess of Kent have her child in Germany, said the Regent, as her sisters-in-law were to do. (Both the Duchess of Clarence and the Duchess of Cambridge were then in Hanover.) Others did not feel the same way, however, and friends rallied to the Duke of Kent's appeals for financial assistance; it was only Edward's threatening to cross the Channel on the common ferry that finally prompted the Regent to agree to send a more suitable ship. But the affair had reached the ears of the Press, and as usual the exchange between the royal brothers was seized upon with delight; there were those who acclaimed

Edward's 'praiseworthy' patriotic wish to have his child born at home, and there were equally others who averred that the birth would be just as legal if it were accomplished abroad.

But Edward had already won his point. True, he was leaving unsettled debts at Amorbach (and after his departure servants were to go unpaid for months and the recent repairs to be allowed to decay), and in England he could face only further calls on his income, but above all else, he would have the satisfaction of an English-born heir. Victoire, too, was pleased with the idea. She had no fears for her health on the journey—Frau Marianne Siebold, a qualified gynaecologist, was to accompany her to superintend the birth. As the day of the departure drew nearer, the Duchess had the consolation of a visit from her mother, still sprightly though now in her sixties. The Dowager Duchess Augusta found her daughter busy and cheerful, indeed, so busy that she did not stay over-long at Amorbach, but having assured herself that her prognostications as to the happiness of the match had proved true, returned home on 24th March.

It was a merry party which set out on the long road to England (some four hundred miles) two days later: the Duke of Kent, living happily for the moment, and for the future gift of a child—for once putting from his mind the thought of his still-mounting debts; the Duchess, enjoying the bustle of travelling after months of enforced sedentary occupations; the nine-year-old Princess Feodora of Leiningen, eager to see foreign places on her first excursion from Germany; faithful Späth, the lady-in-waiting, attentive to her mistress and watchful of the more precious items of luggage; Doctor Siebold, assiduous and possessive, with the pleasing manner which was to further her career as midwife to royalty for some twenty years.

As the cavalcade went slowly north, stopping for rest as often as possible, news came in from Hanover that the Duchess of Cambridge had given birth to a son on 26th March and that on the 27th, the Duchess of Clarence had had a daughter, who lived only a few hours. Until the Kents' child arrived, the new

George of Cambridge was the one heir to the throne in the younger generation; this fact can only have renewed Edward's zeal. He chafed to be home, but it was not until 23rd April, after a four-hour crossing from Calais to Dover in a high wind, that the family arrived in England.

For Edward and Victoire the road to London was broken by an over-night stop at Cobham Hall, the country seat of the Earl of Darnley, but Feodora and the main body of servants went ahead to Kensington Palace, where they welcomed the Duke and Duchess the following day. On the 27th the *Morning Chronicle* was able to assure its readers that "The Duchess of Kent, we are happy, to say, has not experienced the least inconvenience from her journey, and is in the enjoyment of the most excellent health."[17]

Now there was nothing to do but wait.

On 24th May 1819, at four-fifteen in the morning, Frau Siebold, assisted by Doctors Wilson and Davis, delivered the Duchess of Kent of a daughter. Edward had, of course, hoped for a son: with the throne of England in view, a female heir, though eligible, was surely only second-best. He could not foresee that this child was to redeem the British monarchy from years of mediocrity, though the Duke did make an inspired comment on the subject: "As to the circumstance of the child not proving to be a son instead of a daughter, I feel it due to myself to declare that such sentiments are not in unison with my own; for I am decidedly of the opinion that the decrees of Providence are at all times the wisest and best."[18] At all events, there was no reason to suppose that the Duchess would not bear sons in the future.

Back in Germany, the maternal grandmother was similarly satisfied, envisaging future glories for the House of Coburg now united with England. She wrote to her daughter:

I cannot express how happy I am to know you, dearest, dearest Vicky, safe on your bed with a little one, and that all went off so happily. May God's blessings rest on the little stranger and the beloved mother.

Again a Charlotte—destined, perhaps, to play a great part one day, if a brother is not born to take it out of her hands.

The English like Queens, and the niece of the ever-lamented, beloved Charlotte will be most dear to them.

I need not tell you how delighted everybody is here in hearing of your safe confinement. You know that you are much beloved in this your little home.[19]

NOTES TO CHAPTER THREE

1   Augusta, Dowager Duchess of Saxe-Coburg-Saalfeld, *In Napoleonic Days*, p. 189 : 26.5.18.
2   *Ibid.*
3   *Ibid.*, p. 190 : 30.5.18.
4   *Ibid.*, p. 191 : 2.6.18.
5   Stockmar, *Memoirs*, volume i, pp. 75–7.
6   *The Times*, 27.6.18.
7   *Lady's Magazine*, volume 49, p. 337.
8   W. H. Fremantle to the Marquess of Buckingham, 15.7.18 : Buckingham, *Memoirs of the Court during the Regency*, volume ii, p. 267.
9   *Lady's Monthly Museum*, volume viii, p. 122.
10 Stuart, *Mother of Victoria*, p. 36.
11 *The Times*, 17.7.18.
12 *Ibid.*, 20.7.18.
13 Maxwell (ed.), *Creevey Papers*, volume i, p. 283 : 10.9.18.
14 Walter, *Die Kunstbestrebungen des Furstenhauses Leiningen . . .*, p. 24.
15 Edward, Duke of Kent, to Victoire, Duchess of Kent, 31.12.18 : RA M2/73 : Longford, *Victoria R.I.*, p. 24.
16 Edward, Duke of Kent, to Dr Rudge, 19.319 : Neale, *Life of H.R.H. Edward, Duke of Kent*, pp. 266–7.
17 *Morning Chronicle*, 27.4.19.
18 Duff, *Edward of Kent*, p. 267.
19 Augusta, Dowager Duchess of Saxe-Coburg-Saalfeld, to Victoire, Duchess of Kent; Grey, *Early Life of the Prince Consort*, pp. 22–3.

CHAPTER FOUR

"That Dreadful Time at Sidmouth"

Soon after the birth of Edward and Victoire's baby, the prospect of the christening raised the all-important question of the names to be bestowed on the Princess. 'Elizabeth' had a queenly ring to it; 'Charlotte' seemed an obvious, though perhaps not a well-omened choice; 'Augusta' would please the paternal aunt and the maternal grandmother; 'Alexandrina' would be a compliment to the Tsar of Russia, one of the godfathers, and 'Georgiana' to the other, the Prince Regent; 'Victoria', the form of 'Victoire' which the Duchess of Kent was soon to adopt for herself, was a name unprecedented in the royal family, but it was usual to include the mother's name among those of the child. However, family arguments soon whittled the list down to two: Elizabeth, Charlotte and Augusta were first discarded; Georgiana was dropped at the firm insistence of the Regent, who took a fit of pique that a form of his name having to follow that of the Tsar, whom he detested. 'Alexandrina Victoria', though outlandish to English ears, it was to be.

Accounts of the christening suggest that the matter of the names had not been finalized beforehand, but that the Regent and the Duke of Kent quarrelled about them then and there, glowering at each other over the font, while the Duchess of Kent sobbed in the background. It was the culmination of the friction between the brothers which had been carefully kept from the public, but which had been mounting ever since the Kents' return from Germany. Nevertheless, the christening—which took place at Kensington Palace on 24th June 1819—

was a memorable affair with the royal gold font brought from the Tower of London and set up in the grand saloon of the palace, decked with crimson velvet, which had been brought from the Chapel Royal of St James's Palace : the trappings made up for the plain dress of the guests, who had been forbidden by the Regent to wear regimentals or evening-dress. Both the Archbishop of Canterbury and the Bishop of London conducted the service, which was witnessed by most of the royal family (who had to stand proxy for the absent godparents, the Tsar, the Queen of Württemburg and the Dowager Duchess of Coburg). Three days later, Anglican requirements were fulfilled and completed when the Duchess of Kent was publicly 'churched' and took Communion with her husband.

Happily settled at Kensington, the Duchess performed a further duty to society—rather than hand her child over to a wet-nurse (a procedure general among royal and aristocratic mothers, but one which had risks in terms of the baby's health), Victoire fed the baby herself. Edward was delighted that her "performance of the office, most interesting in its nature, has met with the wishes and feelings of society".[1] With self-conscious 'modernity', the parents had the baby vaccinated at ten weeks old.

One of the Duke's first tasks, once the baby was safely started off in life, both spiritually and physically, was to address himself to liquidating, once and forever, his long-outstanding debts. He had lived with them for years; they had restricted (though to no unbearable degree) his life-style; the additions to the bills which had mounted since his marriage had put back his plans for paying it off by the year 1821; 1825 must now be the target. With convenient and pleasant apartments at Kensington, and the run of Leopold's Claremont at his disposal, the Duke's estate at Ealing now seemed superfluous. Accordingly, a simple means of ridding himself of his property occurred to Edward : a lottery, in which each participant would offer a comparatively small sum in the hope of drawing the winning ticket, and by which the sale of many such tickets would raise a price worthy of the house and grounds—a more certain method of achieving their full value than an auction or private sale. But to put the property to a public lottery, the Duke must have the approval of Parliament. Despite the pressure of Edward's friends on his behalf in both Houses (who were mainly men of the Left, like Alderman Wood of London and Joseph Hume, the Radical, and who were few in number among the middle-class and property-conscious capitalists of the mainstream Whig party and non-existent among the Tories), his enemies proved more powerful. Parliament expressed its "unqualified disapprobation" of the scheme at the beginning of July. Nor, resorting to the more mundane means of selling, could Edward raise money on Castle Lodge any other way. Valued at some £53,000, it was an expensive white elephant.

Despite this annoyance, and the pressures on the Duke to make new contrivances to settle his finances, the summer passed pleasantly enough. There was the baby to dandle, and the child Feodora to amuse and instruct (she was quicker than her mother in learning English). It can surely only have been for Feodora's edification that, one day towards the end of the summer, a novel and probably highly dangerous device was brought into the Palace gardens—'Mr Birch's trivector'. This machine was obviously some sort of vehicle, for it was described as having made the journey to London from Brighton under its own power; it was controlled by three men, who manœuvred the 'trivector' round the gardens, followed eagerly by Feodora (with the family doctor in attendance, presumably in case the strange contrivance should run amok and harm anyone).

Feodora also played her part in the celebrations of the Duchess's birthday on 17th August, when she and all the servants roused the Duke and Duchess at six-thirty in the morning, singing God Save the King outside their bedroom door. After such a surprise, the dinner party and concert planned for the evening must have paled into insignificance. And now, since the baby's feeding habits had been regulated, theatre visits were resumed. For example, on 19th July, the Kents went to Covent Garden to see Hamlet and a pantomime called Mother Goose, though, according to the theatre critic of The Times, they must have been disappointed with the latter, which bore no resemblance to the popular original, and was "a strange indescribable farrago". The critic wrote scathingly that "A theatre so liberally patronized as this is by the public should, from a sense of honour, disdain to fill its benches by deluding the readers of its placards with the promise of an entertainment which is not to be performed."[2]

Family parties filled evenings not otherwise engaged: Leopold was back and forth from Claremont; the royal dukes and duchesses exchanged dinners and concerts with the Kents, ever watchful for the first signs of pregnancy in each other. In September, the Clarences came home, still childless, for Adelaide had miscarried at Calais. Here was a woman whose character was as complementary to that of the Duchess of Kent as their appearance had been at their joint wedding. While Victoire was active and often exuberant, Adelaide was quiet and introverted: but she was eager for friendship, and starved of the baby-love which the Kents' child could give her. An intimacy sprang up between the two women, who could chatter in German together and wonder at the strange, temperamental family into which they had married. Victoire found more real warmth there than in Edward's own sisters, who had always laughed at their slightly pompous brother—calling him 'Joseph Surface' after the hypocrite in *The School for Scandal*. The sisters were highly amused when, on a visit to Windsor, the Kents had stood up at nine o'clock in the evening, wished everyone good night and departed to their apartments, followed by Feodora, the lady-in-waiting, the baby and the nurse, and "actually *went to bed*".[3]

By the autumn, Edward was really frightened at the expenses of living in London, and was getting restless for a change. He had never lived in town for any length of time, and was eager to be away. At first, he thought that he might visit his friend Robert Owen, the industrialist-philanthropist who lived in that dreary north country which few members of the royal family had ever cared to see. To Edward, himself no mean student of social conditions, Owen's model village of New Lanark was a lure not to be rejected lightly, but, he reflected, now was not the time to indulge himself with the pleasure of examining its charms. The north, in winter, gave one a memory-picture of that frozen season in Canada. Regretfully, he wrote to his friend thanking him for the hospitality he had offered; plain accommodation was no deterrent, the Duke assured him, rather "what we should prefer to any other",⁴ and though the interest of the trip would more than repay his outlay on it, the main factor in his refusal was the Duchess's current ill-health.

Nevertheless, if Edward could not take his family north, they must go *somewhere* for the winter. In the spring, they would return once more to Amorbach, which would help the strained exchequer, but *now* there must be found a cheap house somewhere in the provinces to relieve the calls on Edward's income in town. He began to look to the clement west for a winter home. In October, he toured the coastal resorts of Devon: Exeter, Torquay, Teignmouth, Dawlish, Exmouth and Sidmouth. At the latter he found what he had been looking for —a secluded cottage, of moderate size and reasonable rent, in a village not yet vulgarized by tourists, where tepid sea-baths could be taken conveniently. Woolbrook Cottage, rented from the mother of General Baynes, would have royal occupants from the end of December.

It was the middle of the month when the Kents set out from Kensington, accompanied by the baby and her nurse, Feodora, and her new German governess, Fräulein Lehzen, Späth the lady-in-waiting, Dr Wilson and Conroy the equerry, besides the necessary, albeit few, servants. With his usual concern for his wife's comfort, Edward had arranged two longish stops along the way. The first was at Windsor to see the Princesses his sisters and—some speculative sources would have one believe—to show the baby to her unhappy grandfather, King George III. The party halted again at Salisbury, at the palace of the Bishop, Dr Fisher, who had been Edward's old tutor as well as being the uncle of Captain Conroy—he had been dubbed 'the Kingfisher' for his obsequious, and successful, attentions to the monarchy. Here in Salisbury, the Duke strode through the precincts and strolled along the aisles of the ancient cathedral, freezing as it was in those winter days, and shivered perhaps with the threat of a feverish cold.

Then, undeterred by the bitter weather that closed in, on they moved to Devonshire. The party arrived at Woolbrook Cottage on Christmas Eve. The first sight of her temporary home must have come as a shock to the Duchess, for it was scarcely a suitable house into which to bring a baby. The cottage was set at the foot of a thickly-wooded valley, with a stream sending up damp mists; it was cold and musty. Even the mild weather the Duke had promised her as being the most favourable factor in their transfer to Devon had failed, and wild gales raged overhead, while a quarter of a mile away the sea broke angrily against the red cliffs. It was an inauspicious beginning to what was soon to prove a tragic episode.

However, Edward retained his faith in Sidmouth, and was soon rewarded. By the end of the month, the gales had blown themselves out, leaving only clean, health-giving winds. The baby seemed to be thriving in the climate—indeed, as the Duke wrote to Wetherall, she was "*too healthy*, I fear, in the opinion of some members of my family, by whom she is regarded as an intruder".[5] And, in view of Edward's misgivings as to the antipathy the mere existence of his daughter aroused (especially, he believed, in the Duke of Cumberland, who coveted the throne and resented his displacement in the succession by the Kent baby), one incident which occurred at Sidmouth at the end of 1819 might have prompted fears of attempted assassination of the baby—though none has ever been proved. One day, after the Duke and Duchess had promenaded for some time with their baby, to the delight of the local inhabitants, the child was brought home to rest. She was lying in the arms of her nurse when a gunshot broke the windows of the nursery, and a bullet whistled past the baby's head. But instead of the expected anarchist or hired killer, the culprit was found to be an apprentice boy potting at birds, who was released from custody at the Duke's request and let off "upon a promise of desisting from such culpable pursuits".[6]

One can only imagine the cries of the baby, the hysteria of the mother and the nurse and the attempts of the father to

soothe them all. He may well have helped to restore tran-
quillity after the first anguished hours by introducing the subject of Amorbach, which was uppermost in his mind, for the
Kents were to go there in a few months' time and arrangements for the journey were already in hand. The Duke was
planning to install teachers there, for the benefit of the poor,
and was still anxious to do his best for his wife's interests in
Germany.

But Edward's plans were to be frustrated. At the very time
at which he was at the height of his happiness and in the full
expectation of a highly pleasant future, fate intervened. The
whole family had taken colds, including Edward, who was
rarely ill and held valetudinarians in contempt. But he could
not deny that his own chill had lasted over-long. Then, on the
13th, he took a walk with Captain Conroy to see the view from
Point Hill—a long walk in the rain. Though, on their return,
Conroy advised him to change his boots, Edward lingered by
the fire, playing with the baby. By the evening, he was hoarse
and shivering, but still refused to take some medicine prescribed
by Dr Wilson. A night's rest, he said, was the best cure.

He was wrong. He had to remain in bed, not now against
his will, for pneumonia was coming on. The doctors who
attended him used the skills that they knew, but these were
barbarous in the extreme—'cuppings' and 'blisterings', which
only drained the strength from the patient. When the worst
fears were confirmed, Prince Leopold was sent for, and so
were Edward's friends Generals Wetherall and Moore. For five
days and nights, Victoire did not leave her husband, not even
changing her clothes, and insisting on giving him his medicine
with her own hands. She was with him when he died, on the
morning of Sunday, 23rd January 1820.

One member of the household unable to give practical help
at the death-bed, but capable of comforting the widowed
Duchess as no other could, was the thirteen-year-old Princess
Feodora of Leiningen, who had come, over the few months of
their acquaintance, sincerely to love her step-father. Forty
years after the event, she wrote to Queen Victoria, her half-
sister: "I well remember that dreadful time at Sidmouth. I

recollect praying on my knees. I loved him dearly; he always was so kind to me. Our dear Mamma was deeply afflicted, but very resigned, and careful not to do you any harm by giving way too much to her grief."[7]

From the moment of Edward's death, the traditional panoply of royalty, which he had scarcely known during his life, was brought into Woolbrook Cottage. In the biggest room of the house, its walls hung with black cloth, lit by candles, the coffin and urn were raised on trestles, covered with a velvet pall. At the head of the coffin, and on either side, were plumes of feathers, and at right and left stood three large wax tapers, in solid silver candlesticks five feet high. For nearly a week, the room was open to visitors, who were regulated by being made to enter by one door and leave by another when paying their respects.

On Monday, the 7th, the funeral cortège began its journey to Windsor, "attended by an immense concourse of spectators, from the surrounding country, who sincerely lamented the early loss of one to whose future residence among them they had looked with the most pleasing sensations".[8] The procession moved slowly, making over-night stops at Bridport, Blandford, Salisbury and Basingstoke, at each place met by gathering crowds, tolling bells and shuttered windows. But the national grief was not entirely for the Duke of Kent: only a few days after Edward had died, his father followed him. In so short a time, the Kents' baby had moved from fifth to third place in the line of succession. Between the child and the crown stood only the ailing new King, George IV, and his two middle-aged brothers of York and Clarence.

At last, on 11th February, the Duke of Kent's funeral cortège reached Windsor. The coffin was carried into St George's Chapel, with the attendance of all members of the royal household and military escort. Seven full Generals bore the Duke's body to the vault. His name and titles were proclaimed for the last time.

Meanwhile, Prince Leopold took charge of his sister and her daughters, escorting them home from Devon. He remembered that time vividly some twenty years later: "That dreary journey, undertaken, I think on the 26th of January, in bitter cold and damp weather, I shall not easily forget. I looked very sharp after the poor little baby, then about eight months old."[9] Denied, by Court etiquette, the consolation of attending her husband's funeral, the Duchess of Kent retired into traditional seclusion.

There was one other person to whom the Duke of Kent's death brought the deepest sorrow—Julie St Laurent, living in Paris. She learned of her former lover's death in a letter from General Wetherall of 23rd January, though that good man had thought to warn her of Edward's illness a few days previously. But no friend of the Duke, however close, could offer condolences more poignant than those of the Duchess herself. Victoire's generous letter to Julie is no longer extant, but a covering note from the Duke of Orleans testifies to its having been sent. Thus, the two women who had shared Edward's life, who had both come to love him for himself, who had never met each other and who were never to do so, shared one point of contact. Julie lived on until August 1830 with only memories of many years with Edward to comfort her; Victoire had his daughter for her consolation.

It must not be supposed that because Edward had not seen Julie for nearly two years before his death that he had forgotten her. He was busy throughout 1818 and 1819 in making financial provision for his former mistress, and took pains to urge his friends to continue the respect that they had shown her under his roof, and to rally round to protect her. At his death, Julie was still in contact with many of them—including the Duke of Orleans who owed Edward for many past favours in his days of exile—and received their comfort as if she had been his legal widow. But then Madame St Laurent passes into obscurity. One source will say that she immured herself in a French convent, another that she returned to Canada, there to marry an Italian prince, Prospero Colonna. A further biographer will maintain that Julie and Edward had had children—offspring of a legal but secret marriage—who were brought up in Canada but who emerged during the reign of Edward's daughter to demand money from her to buy their silence. But the most recent, and comprehensive research, by Mollie Gillen, based upon evidence which brooks little dispute, reveals that Julie lived and died in Paris, and is buried in an overgrown corner of the Père la Chaise cemetery. Few people had known of her association with the Duke of Kent; it was not brought to light until the publication of the *Creevey Papers* in 1903–7. The liaison was the one 'blot' on her father's character that troubled Queen Victoria. In honouring his memory, she preferred to forget Julie St Laurent.

Reactions to the Duke of Kent's death were many and varied. His obituaries in newspapers and magazines were full of praise, glossing over events at Gibraltar or even excusing them, and making much of his charitable interests. His family, also extremely shocked by the death of this little-loved brother (though the blow was overshadowed by the loss of their father), were for once united in pity for his widow and child. Even the Duke of Cumberland managed a kind word. The Princess Augusta was effusive:

> . . . When I think of his poor Miserable Wife and His innocent, Fatherless Child, it really breaks my heart. She has conducted herself like an angel; and I am thankfull [*sic*] Dearest Leopold was with Her. I long to hear of Her; . . . it will be a sad meeting *to us both*. But she will be doubly Dear to me now; and indeed I loved Her sincerely before. She quite adored poor Edward; and they were truly blessed in each other. But what an irreparable loss He must be to Her![10]

In Coburg, the Duchess of Kent's mother was shattered by the news, and was still in the depths of gloom two months after the bereavement, praying God to give her strength to take the loss with resignation and calm.

But inevitably, there were those who could take the blow with equanimity. Frivolous young Louise, Duchess of Saxe-Coburg-Saalfeld, thought only of the tiresome business of going into mourning: "The Duke of Kent has died, suddenly, so *adieu plaisir*."[11] The waspish Countess Lieven, wife of the Russian ambassador in England, had a typically cynical opinion to communicate to her lover, Prince Metternich:

No-one in England will mourn the Duke. He was false, hard and greedy. His so-called good qualities were only for show, and his last public appeal to the charity of the nation had lost him the support of the only friends he had—prisoners and City men. His wife kills all her husbands though. She would cut an interesting figure now if she had it in her to do so; but, whatever you may say, she is the most mediocre person it would be possible to meet.[12]

Somewhere between the eulogies of the obituaries and the assessment by Dorothea Lieven lies the real character of Edward, Duke of Kent. There is no evidence to make him out a saint, but there is none to damn him as a scoundrel; he had the faults of many men and the virtues of as many more. Perhaps he is fortunate in being judged only as a man—had he lived to become King of England, more scrupulous tests must needs have been applied to his character.

NOTES TO CHAPTER FOUR

1   Edward, Duke of Kent, to Dr Collyer, 30.9.19: Neale, *Life of H.R.H. Edward, Duke of Kent*, p. 289.
2   *The Times*, 20.7.19.
3   Mary, Duchess of Gloucester to the Prince Regent, 1819: Stuart, *Mother of Victoria*, p. 88.
4   Edward, Duke of Kent, to Robert Owen: Porter, *Overture to Victoria*, p. 192.
5   Edward, Duke of Kent, to General Wetherall, 29.12.19: Neale, *op. cit.*, p. 289.
6   *Lady's Magazine*, 1820, p. 50.
7   Feodora, Princess of Hohenlohe-Langenburg, to Queen Victoria: Albert, *Queen Victoria's Sister*, p. 34.
8   *Gentleman's Magazine*, volume 90, part i, p. 177.
9   Leopold, King of the Belgians, to Queen Victoria, 22.1.41: Benson and Esher (ed.), *Letters of Queen Victoria*, volume ii, p. 324.
10 Princess Augusta to Lady Harcourt, 1820: Duff, *Edward of Kent*, p. 287.
11 Louise, Duchess of Saxe-Coburg-Saalfeld, to Augusta von Studnitz, 1820: Bolitho, *A biographer's notebook*, p. 114.
12 Countess Lieven to Prince Metternich: Creston, *Youthful Queen Victoria*, p. 85.

CHAPTER FIVE

The Kent Baby

The Duchess of Kent's most immediate problem on the death of her husband was her lack of ready money. Had Prince Leopold not taken charge, Victoire, her children and servants would have had no means even of leaving Sidmouth.

Edward's Will had been made only a short time before his death, by the combined efforts of his brother-in-law, Wetherall, and a Coburg retainer, Edward Stockmar, who had all hastened to Sidmouth as the probability of the Duke's not recovering was known. In a lucid period, though he was still struggling for breath, Edward had gone through his Will twice, before signing it. It read as follows:

> I, Prince Edward, Duke of Kent, being of sound mind, do make my Will, in manner following: And first I do nominate, constitute and appoint my beloved wife, Victoire, Duchess of Kent, to be sole guardian to our dear child, the Princess Alexandrina Victoria, to all intents and for all purposes whatsoever and under a confident hope that my just claim on Government will be yet considered, for the purpose of liquidating my debts, I give, devise, and bequeath unto Frederick Augustus Wetherall, Esquire, Lieutenant and General in the Army, all and every real and personal estates of every sort and nature whatever and wheresoever situate, upon trust, and for the entire use and benefit of my said beloved wife, and dear child, in such manner, on such occasions and at such times, as my said dear wife shall direct. And I do vest the said Frederick Augustus Wetherall and John Conroy, with all and every necessary power and authority, with the consent and approval of my said wife, to dispose of all and

The Palace at Amorbach, from a watercolour *circa* 1820 (reproduced by courtesy of the Amorbach Archives)

(*left*) Edward Augustus, Duke of Kent and Strathearn—Victoire's second husband (reproduced by courtesy of the National Portrait Gallery); (*right*) Emich Charles, Prince of Leiningen—first husband of Victoire—from a portrait at Amorbach (reproduced by courtesy of the Amorbach Archives)

every or any part of my said estate and effects, real and personal, for the purpose before mentioned. And I do hereby constitute and appoint the said Frederick Augustus Wetherall and John Conroy, Executors in trust of this my last Will and Testament. In witness whereof I have subscribed my name, and set my seal, the 22nd day of January, 1820.

EDWARD [1]

But for all the promise of these words—the Duchess would have been heir to nearly £90,000 had all the Duke's assets been realized, and had there been no debts—there was little remaining once provision had been made for the liquidation of the debts. In March, she renounced her interest, and henceforth all moneys from the Duke's estate were to be administered for his creditors. The sale of Castle Lodge, Ealing, would have done much to ease the burden of debt—estimated, in 1821, as having only decreased to £58,664—and in the summer of 1820 attempts were made to sell it. But Castle Lodge did not even warrant its reserved price. It was not until August 1827, at the third attempt to sell the property, that Castle Lodge was at last unloaded. After removing most of the fittings, including even the doors and their frames, the buyer became insolvent before he had paid the full price. In 1829, General Wetherall came to the rescue and completed the purchase of the semi-derelict mansion. It was not until Edward, Duke of Kent's daughter came to the throne that the remaining sum of her father's debt was liquidated.

The Duchess's only income, in those dark winter days of 1820, seemed to be her £6,000 jointure. Had it not been for the allowance made her by her brother Prince Leopold of £2,000 a year (later increased to £3,000), she must have been in dire straits. It was not until 1825 that Parliament was brought to make a more substantial contribution. In May of that year, the Duchess's financial situation was eased by the nation's grant of £6,000 per annum. The general feeling in Parliament by then was that the Duchess had done her duty by her English child, and several complimentary speeches were made. Mr Robinson, Chancellor of the Exchequer, noted that "Perhaps it would have been fit to have brought this matter [of the

E

allowance] before Parliament before."[2] The Duchess would certainly have agreed with him: for the past five years she had owed everything to her brother Leopold, had gone into debt which would take years to pay off and had come to feel that she was being slighted and ignored both by the nation and by her late husband's family.

But she could be sure, then, in 1825, that she had made the right decision at the time of Edward's death, in remaining in England. In that bitter January of 1820, however, the temptation to return home to Germany had been very strong. Staying in England, she would have to resign herself to being almost a pauper, reliant on the charity of her brother; in Germany, she would find a real welcome in the tiny principality of which she was still the ruler, and there she could command both respect and an income in her own right. George IV advised the latter course; in fact, he put pressure on Victoire to leave England: he feared that the widow's presence would bring upon him the representations of his dead brother's friends to increase her income from his own pocket, or even to pay off Edward's debts. But despite the reasonable factors in favour of her return to Germany, the Duchess of Kent paid due attention to her brother's explanation of the situation in England with regard to the baby's inheritance. George IV had had a serious illness within days of his accession: he might well die very soon. Only two old men, both childless, stood between Alexandrina Victoria and her high destiny. The best way of safeguarding the child's future, and of ensuring that if the Princess were called to be Queen, she had a measure of popularity in England, was to stay. Victoire saw the point; she resigned the Leiningen regency, and prepared to settle down. Her decision to stay was to put the King at a distance for years, annoyed that his advice had been ignored, and that he must put up with the frequent reminders of his unconscious heir.

But if the King was cool to the Duchess, the rest of the family was not. Immediately upon Victoire's arrival in London, on 29th January, the Duchess of Clarence hastened to her, to console her in their native German. As Princess Augusta gushed:

In all my own sorrow I cannot yet bear to think of that good, excellent Woman, the Dutchess [*sic*] of Kent, and all her trials; they really are most grievous. She is the most pious, good, resigned little Creature it is possible to describe. She has Written to me once; and I received the letter from Her, and one from Adelaide [the Duchess of Clarence] *Written together* from Kensington. Dearest William [the Duke] is so good hearted, that He has desired Adelaide to go to Kensington every day, as she is a great comfort to the poor Widow; and Her sweet, gentle mind is of great use to the Dutchess of Kent. It is a great delight to me to think that they can read the same *Prayers, and talk the same mother tongue* together; it makes them such real friends and Comforts to each other....[3]

Adelaide had her own problems: her husband's eccentricities, his riotous bastards, her own inability to give him a child; but she continued her visits to Victoire throughout the spring, tempering with discretion her natural joy at her own new pregnancy—for any child, should it live and thrive, must naturally remove the Kent baby one step further down in the line of succession. But, yearning for a child of her own, the Duchess of Clarence adored the precocious 'Drina', as the baby was called (the name Victoria came only later, gradually replacing the nursery diminutive of 'Alexandrina'). From her earliest moments of consciousness, the baby was continually shown pictures of her father, till they became firmly set in her mind, so much so (as the Duchess of Clarence witnessed) that when Drina saw her uncle William wearing his Star decoration, it reminded her of the portraits she had seen: the child stretched out her arms to him, exclaiming "Papa! Papa!"

By the summer, the Duchess of Kent felt able to face strangers once more, and everyone who met her at Kensington was treated to an interview with the royal baby. William Wilberforce, one of the philanthropist friends of the Duke of Kent, was among the first to be granted an audience. Another visitor, Harriet, Countess Granville, found the Duchess of Kent "very pleasing indeed, and raving of her baby. *'C'est mon bonheur, mes delices, mon existence. C'est l'image du feu roi!'* Think of the baby. They say it is the *Roi* George in petticoats, so fat it can scarcely waddle."[4]

But there were threats to the baby's chances of the crown. In December 1820, Adelaide, Duchess of Clarence, redeemed her past failures in child-bearing by giving birth, some weeks prematurely, to a daughter. (More amenable to his brother William than he had been to Edward, George IV allowed the child to take 'Elizabeth' as her first name, graciously permitting a form of his own, 'Georgiana', to follow, with the mother's name added.) For four months, the Princess of Clarence displaced her cousin of Kent in the royal succession; then she died. In August of that year, the Duchess of York had died—totally unmourned, and there was the chance that her widower might find himself a young, nubile bride capable of diverting the ultimate succession to his House—but he was enamoured of a married woman, and preferred to remain out of the race. More serious a proposition was the King, who was finally rid of the erring Caroline of Brunswick by her death in August 1821. He was at first firmly set on acquiring a new wife—but the pleasures of his mature mistresses proved too strong a hold on him. Nevertheless, there were always rumours circulating as to his prospects, which were to disturb the Duchess of Kent until George IV breathed his last.

For the next few years, the Duchess of Kent lived quietly, her life centred on the child on whom her hopes of future grandeur were grounded. The household revolved around the Princess Alexandrina Victoria: the young Princess Feodora rivalled her mother in adoration of the infant; Späth, the lady-in-waiting, Lehzen, the governess, and Mrs Brock, the old nurse, vied for her favours. Though the child was kept closely guarded, occasionally 'the people' might see her in her perambulator on Palace Green, or later walking in Kensington Gardens, clutching the hand of Feodora or her mother. A more inquisitive commoner once observed the family at breakfast beneath the trees of the Palace gardens one summer morning.

These were tranquil days for the Duchess of Kent; days in which to remember past happiness with her husband, so briefly known; days in which to dream of the future, to plan how best to take up her position in the world when Alexandrina Victoria might be called upon the wear the crown which her father had missed.

Links with the family at Coburg remained strong, a proof of attachments formed in childhood. Though Prince Leopold spent only short periods in England in the early 1820s, he was assiduous in giving advice to his sister, and always attentive to the needs of her child. And, in the wider circle which stretched over Germany and into Russia, the network of Coburg correspondence was maintained.

One object of especial interest to the Duchess of Kent was the family of her eldest brother, Ernest (who, in 1825, with the failure of male heirs in the Saxe-Gotha line, exchanged the titles and estates of the dukedom of Saxe-Coburg-Saalfeld for those of the new Saxe-Coburg-Gotha, in a general shuffle of the Saxon states with distant cousins). In August 1817, Victoire, then still Princess of Leiningen, had shared in the family's joyful reception of Ernest's bride, Louise, heiress of Saxe-Gotha, upon whom all doted for her beauty and confiding ways. In the subsequent years, she had borne two sons, Ernest and Albert (the latter a month or so after the birth of his cousin Alexandrina Victoria of Kent). But, in 1824, Louise left the ducal palace never to return, never again to see her sons, disgraced by an *affaire* with a courtier—though her husband's indiscretions were winked at by all. In 1826, the Duke divorced her, and she died, still gay and beautiful, of cancer, aged thirty-one.

The Duchess of Kent was soon to hear from her mother's own lips the details of the family upheavals, and news of the young ones, the children of her brothers and sisters, for in the summer of 1825, the Dowager Duchess Augusta came for a two months' visit to England, bringing with her Charles of Leiningen, Victoire's son by her first marriage. The old lady had been the backbone of the family since the previous century, managing the encumbered finances of her husband, ruling the large number of children and providing for their future when they left the nest; she it was who had doggedly hunted Napoleon, in the worst days of the war, when her son, newly Duke of Coburg, was too ill himself to undertake the mission. As Queen Victoria later recalled, her grandmother was "a most remarkable woman, with a most powerful, energetic, almost masculine mind, accompanied with great tenderness of heart and extreme love for nature. . . . She had fine and expressive blue eyes, with the marked features and long nose of her children and grandchildren."[5]

The great moment of the Dowager Duchess's arrival was to stay with the child Victoria throughout her life:

> I recollect the excitement and anxiety I was in, at this event—going down the great flight of steps to meet her when she got out of the carriage, and hearing her say, when she sat down in her room, and fixed her fine clear blue eyes on her little granddaughter whom she called in her letters "the flower of May", "*Ein schönes Kind*"—"a fine child".[6]

Recently, there came to light the letters which the Duchess Augusta wrote home to her family during her stay in England, which are a delight in themselves for their lively, observant style, and which give a unique insight into the life of the Duchess of Kent during her years of relative obscurity. The old lady was appalled to see the change in her daughter wrought by years of worry and enforced self-reliance: "The poor thing looks so ill and has lost so much weight that I had to force myself not to burst into tears,"[7] she wrote, on meeting her daughter after a six-year separation. Only later in the visit was she able to record that "when she has applied a little rouge, she is still very pretty. . .".

But the highlight of the holiday was first acquaintance with "the May-flower", "the Little Mouse", or, in contrast with her elder half-sister, just "the Little One". The Duchess Augusta wrote of Victoria that "her face is just like her father's, the same artful blue eyes, the same roguish expression when she laughs. She is big and strong as good health itself, friendly and cuddlesome—I would even say obliging—agile, poised, graceful in all her movements. We understand each other fairly well but are on the best of terms."

The child had been taught a little German, but insisted that her grandmother speak to her in English, which the old lady, for all her knowledge of English literature and history, had not perfectly mastered: "When I speak incorrectly, she says quite softly, 'Grandmamma must say . . .' and then tells me how it should be said. Such natural politeness and attentiveness as that child shows has never come my way before."

Again and again in her letters, Augusta returns to the subject of her little grand-daughter, "a beauty, . . . a darling clown". She could never get enough of the child's company, nor cease to marvel at her attractive ways:

Recently, I went out with her, the wind blew my hat to one side. The Little One looked very seriously at Antonia [an attendant] and said "Antonia, my grandmamma's hat doesn't fit properly." In the evening, when she collects me for tea, she quickly runs to the maid and says, "you must extinguish the light."

Since one is six years old with impunity, there is often bargaining whilst going to bed. Then she blames her Sarah, accusing her of hurting her while washing her. In the morning, she sometimes does not want to get out of bed, preferring to tell all sorts of tales. Lehzen [the governess] takes her gently from the bed, and sits her down on the thick carpet, where she has to put on her stockings.

One has to contain oneself not to burst out laughing, when she says in a tragic tone of voice, "Poor Vicky! She is an unhappy child! She just doesn't know which is the right stocking and which is the left! I am an unhappy child!"

The whole series of letters, like the Duchess's *Tagenbuch*, covering the Napoleonic wars, is alive with her shrewd, witty and amusing observations of life around her. She was thrilled to be in England, and the smallest things gave her pleasure. It seemed to her, even on the journey from the coast when she was still 'dazed', that here was a country of gardens such as she had never seen before, and the fashionable 'Gothick' mansions caught her fancy. She was fascinated, from the moment of her arrival, by stage-coaches, which "with their elegant red-uniformed postillions, look like the carriages of the nobility"; for the rest of her time in England, she would look out for them, exclaiming in delight: "I don't want to miss a single stage-coach, because I am so amused by all the people sitting in it."

The Dowager Duchess's cheerful nature made her find delight everywhere, especially in the countryside; in every village, she looked out for the faces of "Miss Emma and poor Miss Taylor and good Miss Bates", her favourite characters in Jane Austen's novels, and, one day in August, a pilgrimage was made to Box Hill (found sadly denuded of its many fine trees by a money-grubbing landlord). Every day, there seemed to be a new sight-seeing excursion to be made, to Hampton Court, the Tower of London, Westminster Abbey, the shops, the great City warehouses, the mansions of the aristocracy, and all the sights so vital to the amusement of a first-time London visitor. The Duchess's descriptive powers paid tribute to all she saw:

We made a delightful trip by carriage to Hampstead, situated on a hill from which one can see the whole town as well as a wide stretch of countryside. In the light of evening, the town looks as if it is shrouded in the red smoke of a conflagration, and we continued via Highgate, and the newest and most beautiful part of the town, Regent Street, which reminded me of Petersburg. . . . In town the gas lighting completely blinds me; it has a glare about it which is unbearable. I look into one of the fairy-like boutiques, my head aches.

The Dowager Duchess's holiday was divided between Claremont and Kensington. At the former, much of the day was spent out of doors, in summer weather that was at once hot and humid. Augusta describes her daily round:

After the English breakfast, at which I sit and perspire, I go into the park. There are not many benches, but I have a walking-stick which converts into a stool, given to me by the Duke of Sussex, which is carried by my servant, and at any spot which I like it is spread out and stands firmly on four feet. . . . I put my work-basket down beside me, and work or read if the spot is especially charming. . . . When the others have their *déjeuner fourchette* at two o'clock, I dine with Vicky. Since Pold always goes out hunting now, for grouse on the heath, I suggested eating with the Little One less punctually, for my stomach revolted. In the afternoons I go for a drive with Feodora or the Little One or one of the ladies

On 17th August, Augusta wrote to her sister Louisa in Germany:

Today, on the birthday of my dear Victoire, I shall not write much. To be here, on her dear birthday, is something that at my age I had no longer counted on; and you, with your soft heart, will imagine how deeply moved I am.

Feodora woke her mother with her sweet voice and the Little One scattered flowers around her. She already prepared yesterday, having dressed all her dolls in their Robes of State, with the help of Lehzen, who is her great love. Feodora, who takes after her mother in attentiveness and in her zeal to give pleasure, decorated the birthday table, before her mother was dressed, with a big ivy wreath and the most beautiful flowers. . . .

But inevitably, the happy summer ended. On 26th September, Augusta wrote for the last time from Claremont:

Like music, the days intermingled with one another, and the eight happy weeks I have spent here have evaporated, a beautiful dream, never to return. Oh, if only the parting with Victoire and the dear Little One were over, and I were already sitting in Calais!

I find that a 'last day' is just too horrible. Already for some days Victoire and I cannot look at each other without crying. I have just been to the garden again, have roamed once again the dear paths, it was so autumnal. On the big lake at the end of the *bosquet*, the wild ducks were screaming as if they wanted to come across the sea with me, everywhere the yellow leaves on the trees were fluttering. . . .

Oh, how painful it all was! I felt the sad 'for the last time' deep in my heart.

Perhaps, at the parting, the Duchess of Kent and her mother realized that they had met 'for the last time'. The Dowager Duchess of Saxe-Coburg-Saalfeld died in 1831, without having repeated her visit to Victoire in England.

NOTES TO CHAPTER FIVE

1   Neale, *Life of H.R.H. Edward, Duke of Kent*, pp. 302–3.
2   Benson and Esher (ed.), *Letters of Queen Victoria*, volume i, p. 9.
3   Princess Augusta to Lady Harcourt, 4.2.20: Duff, *Edward of Kent*, p. 290.

4 Harriet, Lady Granville, August 1820: Gurney, *Childhood of Queen Victoria*, p. 67.
5 Benson and Esher (ed.), *op. cit.*, volume i, p. 6.
6 and all subsequent quotations, from Cathcart, *Royal Bedside Book*, pp. 14–28.

CHAPTER SIX

The Regency Bill

These were tranquil years for the Duchess of Kent, years of small pleasures and modest entertainments, mainly confined to the family circle. But if she enjoyed retirement and a humdrum daily round, her lively teenaged daughter Feodora did not. Kensington Palace was to her a prison, with its elderly inmates her gaolers. Besides her mother, the lady-in-waiting Späth and the governess Lehzen, her circle of acquaintances comprised few more than the ageing royal princesses, for there was a dearth of suitable young companions. Feodora came to hate Kensington over the years, finding pleasure only in the brief visits to her uncle Leopold's house at Claremont. She wrote, years later:

Claremont is a dear quiet place; to me also the recollection of the few pleasant days I spent during my youth. I always left Claremont with tears for Kensington Palace. When I look back upon those years, which ought to have been the happiest in my life, from fourteen to twenty, I cannot help pitying myself. Not to have enjoyed the pleasures of youth is nothing, but to have been deprived of all intercourse, and not one cheerful thought in that dismal existence of ours was very hard.[1]

But the 'imprisonment' which Feodora endured was a sensible precaution taken by her mother to protect her from the notorious profligacy of George IV's court, and to avoid there being the slightest hint of scandal which would certainly mar her chance of a good marriage. However, despite the Duchess's care, such a scandal nearly occurred in the winter of 1825–6, involving Feodora and the son of the Duke of Sussex, Augustus d'Este.

Augustus was Sussex's son by his morganatic wife, Lady Augusta Murray—that is, he enjoyed the position of an acknowledged and legitimate son of a royal duke, but without the honours and potential inheritance which an officially-recognized marriage of his parents would have given him. He could inherit neither the dukedom of Sussex, nor, if it came to that, the crown. His father was one of the inmates of Kensington Palace, usually one of the members of the small family dinner-parties at which Feodora, 'coming out', was introduced to society. The Duchess Augusta of Coburg, on her visit to England in the summer of 1825, had met the Sussex family, and had summed up Lord Augustus as "pretty and conceited", yet already perhaps the young Feodora admired him. She was only seventeen, he thirty-one, a fine figure in his colonel's uniform.

That autumn, they met secretly; they exchanged letters. His intentions seemed honourable, however, for he asserted to her that there could be no objections to their marriage on the grounds of his inferior birth, emphasizing, "the prudent but never ceasing exertions for the ultimate obtaining of those rights which the iron hand of power so unjustly has hitherto withheld for I trust I need not now tell you that I am as legitimate a Prince as any to be named in either of our houses".[2] For all his good looks and determined wooing, Augustus was a sad hypochondriac. As the pace quickened, he noted carefully every increasing mark of ill-health, caused by the strain: "I sometimes imagined spots floating before my eyes."[3]

But if the thrills of clandestine courtship were too much for Augustus, they also claimed their toll from Feodora: when he sent her two gold rings, via the *intriguante* Späth, she panicked. She told her mother everything. The Duchess ordered her daughter to break off all relations, and the rings were returned by Späth before the angry mother could hear of their existence. The Duke of Sussex was then told of the affair. He brought his presumptuous son to task in no uncertain terms. Augustus records: "In the month of January 1826 the most painful

Chapter up to that period of my life occurred, I was beset by afflictions on all sides. My Eyes were again attacked. . . . The causes of my afflictions continued, but their effects were somewhat mitigated by time."[4] If Feodora suffered equally, there is no evidence of it.

With Augustus d'Este safely packed off to Germany—for his health, the Duchess of Kent might have had an easier mind. But in the summer of 1826, her elder daughter was beginning to attract attention in a higher quarter. Feodora's grandmother in Coburg noted: "I see by the English newspapers that 'His Majesty and H.R.H. the Duchess of Kent went on Virginia Water'. The little monkey must have pleased and amused him. She is such a pretty, clever child. The bigger monkey was always much in favour."[5] The 'little monkey', sharp-eyed, seven-year-old Victoria, had observed that on this occasion the 'bigger monkey', Feodora, was getting the lion's share of the King's favours: "The King paid great attention to my Sister, and some people fancied he might marry her!! She was very lovely then—about 18—and had charming manners, about which the King was extremely particular."[6] The Duchess of Kent was really frightened: she could easily envisage the situation by which Feodora's marriage to George IV would relegate herself to the role of mother of the Queen Consort, instead of that of mother to the Queen Regnant which she fully expected one day to enjoy. George could not live much longer (in fact he died in 1830) and she would then be left in the obscure position of grandmother to his heir, the potential child of Feodora. This was not what she had given up so much for seven long years to obtain.

Thus, while the Duchess maintained outward amity with the King, consulting him on matters of Victoria's health and education, she was privately arranging with her mother for Feodora to visit her in Germany. In the autumn, Feodora left England, with her uncle Leopold to chaperone her on the journey. She was dutiful and obedient in going—but she could not be kept away for ever.

When Feodora returned to England, the situation with the King had not materially improved, in her mother's opinion.

The summer of 1827 was fraught, as the Duchess attempted to keep the Princess away from London. She used the excuse of Victoria's need to recuperate from a vaccination in early July, to take her daughters on holiday in the southern counties, where they were joined by her son Charles. Then came a new development—which the Duchess interpreted in her own way: George created her household Comptroller, Conroy, a Knight Commander of a Hanoverian order and the governess Lehzen a baroness. What could this be more than a bribe for their assistance to his suit when the time came, and a sweetener to herself? The Duchess, in acknowledging the King's marks of favour, wrote: "I am embarrassed and at a loss how I can express, *as I feel*, the deep sense I entertain of your Majesty's graciousness: I am sensible of the favor you have shown Miss Lehzen; who is all gratitude!"[7] After all, she could scarcely reveal her suspicions of her brother-in-law's motives to such generosity. But her letter to George does conclude with the words: "Feodora is quite flattered with your Majesty's constant recollections of her."[8]

Returning to Kensington Palace in the autumn, the Duchess of Kent made swift plans to prevent her elder daughter from harming the inheritance of her youngest child, by arranging a suitable German marriage for her. It was a match to which no one could reasonably object. The young man chosen was Prince Ernest of Hohenlohe-Langenburg, thirty-two years old, heir to an old title and good estates, President of the Upper House of Württemburg. He had met the Princess during her visit to Germany the previous winter. Now the match was arranged with the help of Adelaide, Duchess of Clarence, his first cousin, and in January 1828, Ernest presented himself in London as Adelaide's guest. George IV had to forget his own hopes when faced with this *fait accompli*. He was so gracious as to receive the Prince on 7th February.

On the 15th, the Duchess of Kent gave one of the biggest receptions she had attempted since her widowhood. *The Times* reported:

The company began to arrive at the Palace soon after nine o'clock. The Great Hall was brilliantly illuminated. In the sub-hall the band of the 3d Regiment of Foot Guards, in full uniform, were stationed in an orange shrubbery, surrounded with a variety of trees, plants and flowers. The band played some overtures and other pieces of music during the night, and received the different branches of the Royal Family on their arrival with *God Save the King*.

The whole of the Duchess's apartments were thrown open, and were splendidly illuminated. The Duchess received her Royal and distinguished visitors in the Saloon.[9]

The next day, Saturday, the Duchess of Kent gave a more select family dinner, during which her son Charles arrived from the Continent. Then, on Monday, came the wedding. Crowds gathered outside Kensington Palace in expectation of seeing the King, who was to give the bride away, and the bells of the parish church pealed merrily throughout the day. But the service was to take place within the Palace, where a temporary altar had been fitted up, with Dr Kuper, the chaplain of the Royal German Chapel, to conduct the ceremony according to the Lutheran rite. At three o'clock the wedding began—but with the Duke of Clarence leading in Feodora, instead of his brother who had sent word that he was unable to attend.

Both Feodora and her little sister Victoria, her bridesmaid, were dressed in materials of entirely British manufacture, the wedding gown being made of Buckinghamshire thread lace. The guests and the servants were decked out in "favours of the largest size",[10] that is, coloured ribbons and flowers, which the little Princess Victoria distributed to them from her basket. Many years later Feodora wrote to her on the anniversary of her wedding-day :

I always see you, dearest, little girl as you were, dressed in white—which precious lace dress I possess now—going round with the basket presenting the favours. That was a day of happiness and pain at the same time for your poor sister. How good it is that in youth one is so light-hearted . . . there is still always such hope and elasticity in one's thoughts and feelings. To me hope has not been treacherous; on the contrary, I have found much more happiness than I ever thought of possessing.[11]

But Feodora had not the benefit of that foresight of happiness when she drove away from Kensington with her bridegroom at eight o'clock on her wedding-day, to go to Claremont. However, if she was nervous at being alone with Ernest for the first time, sheltered as she had been in an almost entirely female household, she was not to be left *tête-à-tête* for long. The next day, her mother, Victoria and Charles joined them at Claremont, and the following Thursday, they accompanied the couple to Windsor to see the King—doubtless to thank him for his gift of a diamond necklet to the bride. Did Feodora give it a thought that had George been encouraged to sue for her hand himself, she might now have been *his* wife, and enjoying the use of the Crown Jewels, and the personal adornments of the sovereign's consort?

On the Saturday, the Hohenlohes returned to Kensington Palace, then, on Tuesday the 26th, after another night at Claremont, set off for Germany. Their ship left England on the morning tide of the 27th.

Despite the physical distance between them, and the infrequency of their meetings, Feodora and her sister remained close in sympathy. Indeed, the bond between the Duchess's three children was remarkably strong. Victoria wrote: "We three were particularly fond of each other, and never felt or fancied that we were not real *Geschwister* [children of the same parents]. We knew but one parent, our mother, so became very closely united, and as I grew up the distance which difference of age placed between us entirely vanished."[12]

Though Feodora had satisfied her mother, had been acquiescent to her plans and dutiful in carrying them through, her brother Charles was not so passive. When his grandmother had brought him to England in 1825, both she and the Duchess of Kent had hoped that his holiday night lead him to forget the *inamorata* he had left behind. The lady was one Marie Klebelsberg, a thoroughly ineligible *partie* with whom young Charles was infatuated. Marie had been introduced to the Coburg circle by Duke Ernest's wife, Louise, who had met the Klebelsbergs while on a spa holiday in Germany. She had been charmed by the pretty girl and had taken her into her household. When Duchess Louise left her husband in 1824, the old Dowager Duchess had taken pity on Marie and had made her her lady-in-waiting. Charles Leiningen found her irresistible. Despite his family's remonstrances that she was of inferior rank (the daughter of a count), he went his own way, and in February 1829 he married her.

During the decade since the Duke of Kent had begun to improve the palace at Amorbach, it had once again fallen into disrepair. Only a few months after his marriage, however, Charles began to rebuild. His finances came from one source: his mother. For seven years, she was to send large sums to her son from her own scarcely-adequate income. He repaired and refurnished Amorbach to the tune of about £22,500, and rebuilt the hunting-lodge of Waldleiningen, some eight miles from Amorbach, on a grand scale. Though Charles never repaid the Duchess, she had her reward very soon in the shape of grand-children—first the heir to the principality, Ernest, born in November 1830, then another boy, Edward, in 1833.

Now, with her two elder children settled and happy, the Duchess of Kent could concentrate on furthering the chances of the Princess Victoria, as time brought the crown of England ever closer.

The year 1830 was a turning-point in the lives of both Victoria (as she was, by now, signing herself), Duchess of Kent and Princess Victoria, her daughter. And perhaps the moment has come for an appraisal of the elder Victoria's character.

She has been seen first as the dutiful daughter, marrying the man of her parents' choice, the Prince of Leiningen. As his wife, she has earned the praise of her own mother as a good home-maker in a trying situation. She has been seen to merit, and has gained, the guardianship of her son at a time in which few women would have been considered capable of the task. In considering a second marriage—one which many women would have found irrestistibly attractive—she has waited to accept the proposal until the welfare of her children has been ensured. In her second marriage, she has made her husband happy (against the odds of a rival, deeper attachment) and has promptly provided him with the *raison-d'être* of the marriage, a child. At his death-bed she has acted with exemplary solicitude. Given the chance of returning to her native land, she has chosen to remain in England for the sake of her child's birthright. She has reared that child in good health.

So far, she has been the pattern of filial, connubial and maternal duty, but her character is still flat. Only the rival claims on her ambition of Feodora and Victoria give a slight clue to her thoughts and motives. For the rest, they lie hidden; 1830 and the subsequent years will, however, provide tests which open up the personality of Victoria, Duchess of Kent, though they will more often pose questions and complications than they will offer answers and clarifications.

As 1830 progressed, it became obvious that George IV was dying. His death would bring Princess Victoria (who celebrated her eleventh birthday in May) one step closer to the throne, to the position of heiress presumptive. Between her and her destiny stood only William, Duke of Clarence, himself in his fifties, whose wife was now unlikely to give him the heir who would dispossess Victoria. (The Duke of York had died in 1827.) The time had come, therefore, to prepare the child for the shock of her future career, which had hitherto never occurred to her and which had been kept from her by her relations. The scene of the enlightenment is famous—if debatably apocryphal: during a history lesson Victoria scans a family tree of the royal line; suddenly she notices her own name close to that of the King; the realization dawns; the well-brought-up, serious child vows "I will be good". Yet after all the years of concealment, this discovery was no accident. It had been carefully prepared and timed, taking place, according to tradition, on 11th March 1830. On the first day of the month, the Duchess of Kent had taken her first step towards gaining her Grand Design—a regency for her daughter, should both George IV and his brother William die before the girl had gained her majority (the age of eighteen): she had placed before the Bishops of London and Lincoln the curriculum of studies she had prescribed for Victoria, soliciting their approval. In the preamble to the table of lessons, the Duchess wrote:

The Princess will be eleven years of age in May; by the death of her revered father when she was but eight months old, her sole care and charge devolved to me. Stranger as I then was, I became deeply impressed with the absolute necessity of bringing her up entirely in this country, that every feeling should be that of Her native land, and proving thereby my devotion to duty by rejecting all those feelings of home and kindred that divided my heart.[13]

The Duchess reminded the divines that

At the present moment no concern can be more momentous, or in which the consequences, the interests of the Country, can be more at stake, than the education of its future Sovereign.

I feel the time to be now come that what has been done should be put to some test, that if anything has been done in error of judgment it may be corrected, and that the plan for the future should be open to consideration and revision. I do not presume to have an over-confidence in what I have done; on the contrary, as a female, as a stranger (but only in birth, as I feel that this is my country by the duties I fulfil, and the support I receive), I naturally desire to have a candid opinion from authorities competent to give one.[14]

The appeal was eloquent and invoked sympathy. The tutor's scheme of studies was competent and broad. The Bishops questioned Victoria on her religion. A report was made out, which was passed on to the Archbishop of Canterbury. All were satisfied.

Thus, the Duchess had proved to independent and unimpeachable witnesses her fitness to continue the guardianship of her daughter, and had prepared the ground for acceptance as her Regent. Yet she still felt that she had reason to fear rivals, should the matter arise—the Duke of Cumberland perhaps, who would become King of Hanover, by Salic Law which forbade female inheritance, as successor to his brothers George and William. There was nothing she could do, however, until the moment was ripe.

In a letter written for the Princess Victoria's birthday that year, the Duchess's mother expressed pious sentiments that well-accorded with her daughter's more worldly plans:

My blessings and good wishes for the day that gave you the sweet blossom of May! May God preserve and protect the valuable life of that lovely flower from all the dangers that will beset her mind and heart! The rays of the sun are scorching at the height to which she may one day attain. It is only by the blessing of God that all the fine qualities He has put into that young soul can be kept pure and untarnished. How well I can sympathize with the feelings of anxiety that must possess you when that time comes. God who has helped you through so many bitter hours of grief, will be your help still. Put your trust in Him.[15]

The Duchess had not long to wait. George IV died on 26th June 1830. His reign and his regency together had been no more than twenty years. 'The Prince of Pleasure' had left a more characteristic memorial in the buildings he had commissioned than in the legislation of his Parliaments. Few mourned him, certainly not the Duchess of Kent who had felt the spite of his tongue, even though the last few years had brought a truce in hostilities.

The new King, William IV, was not the imposing figure that his brother had been. In the years before he came to the throne, he had done little to earn the nation's contempt, but he had not done much to earn its respect. Without legitimate children of his own, he was prepared to welcome the young Victoria and her mother at his Court, as his acknowledged heir: he had reckoned without the Duchess's prudery at the thought of her child consorting with the King's numerous bastards, and her concern that she should not be 'contaminated' by their company. Close involvement in the private life of the new Court was as taboo as that with the old. Only on formal occasions, such as the Queen's Drawing-Room receptions, would the Princess be paraded with her family.

The regency was now a matter of some urgency. Rumours had started flying as to the contenders in the stakes to govern the potential child-Queen. The worst gossips of the age did not scruple to give their opinions, and spread their witty malice. Neither the Duchess of Kent nor her brother Leopold was spared. Thus the diarist Creevey: "I suppose Mrs Kent thinks her daughter's reign is coming on apace, and that her brother may be of use to her as *versus* Cumberland. . . . Lord Durham is now Prime Minister to the Duchess of Kent and Queen Victoria, and they are getting up all their arrangements together. . . ."[16] And Princess Lieven: "The Duchess of Kent and her brother hold themselves very high, as if the throne is to be theirs tomorrow—and this is most unpleasant to the King. Leopold does not show himself, but works silently underground."[17]

In the autumn, the Regency Bill went to Parliament. In championing it, Lord Chancellor Lyndhurst said:

> It would be quite impossible, that we should recommend any other individual for that high office, than the illustrious Princess, the mother of Her Royal Highness the Princess Victoria. The manner in which Her Royal Highness the Duchess of Kent has hitherto discharged her duty in the education of her illustrious offspring—and I speak upon the subject, not from vague report, but from accurate information—gives us the best ground to hope favourably of Her Royal Highness's future conduct. *Looking at the past, it is evident that we cannot find a better guardian for the time to come.*[18]

The Bill passed into law. In case of the death of King William before 20th May 1837, on which date the Princess Victoria would be eighteen, the Duchess of Kent would be her Regent; an additional £10,000 a year would signify Parliament's acknowledgement of her increased responsibility. But even in her triumph, the Duchess knew the bitterness of defeat. She had not gained the coveted title of Dowager Princess of Wales (to which she had not a shred of right); for the present she was not to be admitted to the Councils of State (nor was she ever to be, in fact). She must find new ways of asserting her claims, of establishing her position in the eyes of the public, of assuring her glorious future.

What is it that divides a mother's anxiety that no one but herself should have the care of her daughter, from that same woman's desire to isolate her daughter for her own advantage? Where does maternal concern end and self-interest begin? Anyone might argue that so capable and shrewd a woman as the Duchess of Kent was a fit person to rule on her child's behalf, and she surely cannot be blamed for wishing to test her powers in a role which all her past life had taught her to consider as of the highest desirability. Victoria, Duchess of Kent might easily be forgiven for scheming to gain the regency to protect her daughter, but there will always be those who will castigate her for the very human motive of personal ambition.

Yet, there is every reason to believe that the Duchess of Kent honestly feared that her daughter stood in need of protection, both physical and moral. She was led to fear that the Duke of Cumberland (a viable alternative to herself as Regent) would be the worst possible guardian of her daughter—that he actually had designs on Victoria's life. The person who encouraged these fears, who insinuated and hinted that the Duchess stood alone among the royal family in cherishing her daughter's claim, was Sir John Conroy, met briefly already as the Duke of Kent's equerry, his companion on that ill-fated Sidmouth visit, the executor of his Will and the Comptroller of the Household of the Duchess of Kent, ever since her widowhood.

Conroy was Irish in antecedence, but born in Wales, where his father had an estate. With little money or influence behind him, he had embarked, in his teens, on a career in the army, and had overcome both his handicaps by marrying, in 1808, Elizabeth Fisher, the daughter—and heiress—of his commanding officer. By the time that General Fisher died, however—causing Conroy to lose his 'pull' with promotions boards—the sharp young man had attached himself to the Duke of Kent. His wife's uncle, the Bishop of Salisbury, had been the means of attracting the Duke's attention to Conroy. Though the Duke could do nothing for his protégé in the army itself, he was able to second him to his own household staff just prior to his marriage to Victoire. Conroy was still in the Kent service nearly twenty years after his patron's death.

In the first years of the Duchess's widowhood, Conroy had made himself indispensable to her. He and his wife, and their young family (one of the girls named Victoire, the eldest boy Edward) were in almost daily attendance on the Duchess. Of necessity thoroughly acquainted with all the Duchess's business, he aligned himself with her interests. She, lonely and in need of masculine guidance, looked increasingly to Conroy for support. Besides, he was nearer to her in age than either of her husbands had been, and possessed of great charm and good looks. Conroy soon established a high degree of influence over her.

It has been asserted that Conroy sincerely believed in the ill-intentions of the Duke of Cumberland; it is more likely, however, in view of the character which he reveals in the years 1830–9, that he exaggerated the rumours of danger in order to isolate the Duchess from the royal family, so that she should rely more on him alone. He also aimed at convincing her of the necessity of keeping her daughter away from her relations, lest any one of them should manage to woo the child away from her mother (and thus from his own power). It was for this reason that Feodora's governess, Louise Lehzen, had been kept at Kensington as the child's governess; as a German, far from home and dependant on the Duchess for continued employment, and for a good reference at its termination, she must surely comply with all Conroy's directives. When the Duchess of Northumberland was appointed 'State Governess' to the Princess, in 1830, her position was intended to be entirely formal and decorative, but, unfortunately for the Conroy regime, she had some curiosity about the upbringing of her charge, and 'interfered' with opinions and suggestions. As soon as was decently possible, when the Princess was confirmed, and deemed to be beyond the need of a governess, the Duchess of Northumberland was dismissed. In addition to her isolation from all but the Kensington circle, the young Princess was kept closely guarded: she slept in her mother's bed each night, she was always led by the hand on the stairs, she was never allowed a moment's solitude.

Despite her dislike of Sir John Conroy (he was knighted in 1827), Princess Victoria was subjected to his company almost every day for the whole of her childhood and adolescence. One of the most often-repeated sentences in her journal is "Sir John dined here". His family too played a prominent part as regular company at Kensington Palace: Lady Conroy was 'delicate', keeping mainly to her sofa, but not averse to the occasional opera outing, but her daughters Jane and Victoire were always in evidence as playmates and dancing-partners of the little Princess. Yet it is noticeable that even Victoire Conroy, Victoria's almost sole companion for some years, is never "dear Victoire" in the Princess's diary, though the adjective is applied indiscriminately to favoured friends and animals, and became "Miss Conroy" as Victoria assumed teenage airs.

It is a great tribute therefore to the dog Flush that it won a place in Victoria's heart, for it was the gift of Sir John Conroy (originally to the Duchess, but appropriated by Victoria before long). Flush's charm must have been great indeed to have overcome Victoria's dislike of the donor.

The gossip which marked Conroy as the Duchess of Kent's lover does not seem to have been in currency much before 1830. Until then, there is no evidence that anyone thought more of his position than his office warranted. Years later, the diarist Charles Greville discussed those early rumours with the Duke of Wellington, who was convinced that there was more in the relationship than met the eye. Wellington told Greville that the Princess Victoria had come upon a love-scene between the Duchess and Conroy:

What She had seen She repeated to the Baroness Spaeth [sic], and Spaeth not only did not hold her tongue but . . . remonstrated with the Duchess herself on the subject. The consequence was that they got rid of Spaeth, and they would have got rid of Letzen [sic] too if they had been able; but Letzen, who knew very well what was going on, was prudent enough not to commit herself, and She was besides powerfully protected by George 4th and Wm. 4th so that they did not dare to attempt to expel her.[19]

Whether that story is exactly true or not, it is indisputable that Späth was despatched to Germany to live with Princess Feodora in 1829, and that the governess maintained the coolest of relations with Sir John after the departure of her bosom friend.

And yet, when the Greville diaries were published for the first time in 1877, Victoria, now Queen, was indignant on her mother's behalf—not only putting on a bland public face, but denying the charge with vehemence in private circles. She held staunchly that her mother, devout and pious, was incapable of such heinous behaviour, and that Sir John, for all his faults, was devoted to his wife. The truth of the situation was most probably that a long-standing flirtation existed between the Duchess and Conroy, which stopped short at a few kisses (witnessed by Victoria), compliments and the delightful attentions which spiced the Duchess's years of deprivation of masculine company. Her current position was too precarious and her future position too tempting for either to be hazarded in a love-affair, which, if discovered, must certainly have led to her disqualification from the Regency in favour of Cumberland. The latter would surely not have scrupled at revealing such an affaire to further his own claim, had there been any evidence (a retirement from Kensington by Lady Conroy, or eye-witness accounts of familiarities by royal servants) to back up contemporary rumours against the Duchess of Kent. And, again, Queen Victoria's letters to her mother at the time of Conroy's death show that she, the most ardent censurist of others' immorality, had no criticism to level at her mother's behaviour, other than that of being too much under Conroy's influence.

Those members of the Court who visited Kensington Palace would notice the ubiquity of Sir John and (eager for some scandal in the dull, respectable Court of the reformed William IV) make more of the matter than the facts would properly allow. Scandal-mongers were later to impute to Queen Adelaide, the most unimpeachable of faithful wives, an adultery with Lord Howe, her Chamberlain. If the Queen, in the open gaze of the Court, could be so maligned, it was easier by far to vilify the Duchess of Kent in the seclusion of Kensington Palace. But while there can be no reason to believe that Conroy was the Duchess's lover, there can be no doubt but that she was completely in his power. He would use her weakness, fears and indecision, as well as her ambition, to advance himself; he would put in her mind all manner of doubts as to her daughter's personal fitness to rule without their guidance; he would aspire to become an *eminence grise*.

One reason for the Duchess's reliance on Conroy was her growing away from the influence of her brother Leopold, completed, after 1831, by his long absence from England. Throughout the 1820s, Leopold had made extensive Continental trips, but had always kept in close touch with his sister to advise her at crucial moments in her career, and had supervised her actions during the Regency debate. But the thin end of the wedge was Leopold's liaison with one Caroline Bauer, a Coburg girl who bore a remarkable resemblance to the late Princess Charlotte, and whose presence in her brother's household sincerely shocked the Duchess of Kent. Then, in 1830, having already turned down the offer of the throne of Greece, Leopold accepted the invitation to become King of the newly-created kingdom of 'Belgium'. His acceptance of the crown marked the beginning of the four years' absence from England which enabled Conroy to establish his ascendancy over the Duchess. Devoted as Leopold was to his sister, and assiduous in his correspondence with her and his niece, he could not counteract forces in the Duchess's life which were so much nearer home than his own.

The little 'prisoner of Kensington Palace', though seemingly surrounded by the devotion and care of all with whom she lived, was now caught in the toils of the man who would at length alienate her from her mother, bully and humiliate her and for a time put in jeopardy her succession to the crown of England. The Princess Victoria, as the 1830s opened, was just coming to realize her predicament—but she was by no means afraid of the future.

Her main asset was her governess, Lehzen, whose position was, on the surface, hazardous: at the mercy of the Duchess and Conroy's tolerance of her opposition to their regime. In fact, her powerful protector was the King, who recognized her harmlessness politically, and her usefulness as a countermeasure against the Duchess. Louise Lehzen, the pastor's daughter from Hanover, in her mid-thirties, was the mistress of shrewd cunning, and could keep observances of '*la politesse*' between herself and her employer, while at the same time enlightening her charge as to her mother's failings; she could also teach the Princess Victoria to maintain the right tone of aloofness to Conroy.

With such an able mentor, and with her own innate royal 'presence' and her Hanoverian temper, Victoria kept up a cool opposition to her imposed regime. Occasionally, she might show some affection for her mother; she would always observe the rules of Biblical 'honour' towards her; but from her teens, Victoria would never allow an infringement of her rights—usually from the direction of Conroy—to pass unprotested. If daily life, the round of lessons, drives and evening entertainments, was generally harmonious within the household, occasionally—then, as the years passed, with increasing frequency—there would be outbursts, recriminations and painful silences between Victoria and her mother. And at the root of them all was Conroy.

NOTES TO CHAPTER SIX

1 Feodora, Princess of Hohenlohe-Langenburg, to Queen Victoria, 1843 : Benson and Esher (ed.), *Letters of Queen Victoria*, volume i, p. 18.
2 Lord Augustus d'Este to Princess Feodora of Leiningen, 1825; Firth, *The case of Augustus d'Este*, p. 21.
3 D'Este MS, p. 2 (Royal College of Physicians).
4 *Ibid.*, p. 3.
5 Augusta, Dowager Duchess of Saxe-Coburg-Saalfeld, to Victoria, Duchess of Kent, 17.8.26 : Grey, *Early Life of the Prince Consort*, p. 47.
6 Benson and Esher (ed.), *op. cit.*, volume i, p. 12.
7 Victoria, Duchess of Kent, to George IV, 14.9.27 : Aspinall (ed.), *Letters of George IV*, volume iii, p. 296.
8 *Ibid.*
9 *The Times*, 16.2.28.
10 *Ibid.*, 19.2.28.
11 Feodora, Princess of Hohenlohe-Langenburg, to Princess Victoria, 4.3.36 : Albert, *Queen Victoria's Sister*, p. 55.
12 Tulloch, *Story of the Life of Queen Victoria*, p. 7.
13 Benson and Esher (ed.), *op. cit.*, volume i, from pp. 14–16.
14 *Ibid.*
15 Augusta, Dowager Duchess of Saxe-Coburg-Saalfeld, to Victoria, Duchess of Kent, May 1830 : Grey, *op. cit.*, p. 54.
16 Maxwell (ed.), *Creevey Papers*, volume ii, part i, p. 210: 26.5.30.

17 Princess Lieven, 1830: Richardson, *My Dearest Uncle*, p. 103.
18 The Lord Chancellor in the House of Lords, 15.11.30: Neale, *Life of H.R.H. Edward, Duke of Kent*, p. 24.
19 Strachey and Fulford (ed.), *Greville Memoirs*, volume iii, p. 177: 8.9.31.

CHAPTER SEVEN

A State of Cold War

Almost immediately upon the accession of William IV, and with the new-found assurance of the Duchess of Kent in her position of Regent-elect, a state of cold war—occasionally flaring into open conflict—broke out between them. The new King was aged sixty-seven, was rarely free from ill-health and was considered by many of his closest associates to be bordering on senility. It was thought unlikely that his reign would be a long one. But the Princess Victoria celebrated only her eleventh birthday in 1830, so that there were full seven years before she might rule without a regency. Thus the Duchess of Kent was eager to establish herself, through her daughter, through political means, publicity and word-of-mouth reports among the small circle of aristocracy and the wider world of 'the people' alike. At the same time, however, the old scheme of isolating the Princess from any outside influence was to be kept up—indeed strengthened.

The main aim was to keep King William and his wife from rivalling the Duchess in the Princess's affections. Though both were eager to make much of their niece, and to have her seen at their Court as often as possible, their plans were thwarted by the Duchess of Kent. Victoria was allowed a place in the mourning train of her uncle George at the Court assembly, but was not permitted to attend the Coronation of her uncle William. When plans were set in train, in the spring of 1831, for the Coronation that September, it was found that Princess Victoria was to follow her uncles in the order of precedence in processions, instead of leading them in her role of heiress presumptive. When all the Duchess's protests were ignored, she decided that her daughter should not attend. She used the excuse of Victoria's ill-health as the plea for her absence.

Inevitably, there was an outcry from the Press, in which *The Times* was at its most scurrilous:

It is with deep regret that we have learned that her Royal Highness [the Duchess] has refused to attend, and that her absence on this occasion is *in pursuance of a systematic opposition on the part of her Royal Highness to all the feelings of the present king.* Now the presence or absence of the Duchess herself is a matter of *comparative* indifference, it is *merely disrespectful*; but that of the Princess Victoria, which must, as to its immediate cause, be imputed to her mother, cannot fail of being considered by the public as *indecent and offensive.* We should be glad to know who are the advisers of this misguided lady? Who can have dared to counsel *her, the widow of a mediatized German prince,* whose highest ambition could never have contemplated the possibility of an alliance with the blood-royal of England, to oppose the sovereign to whom she is *bound by so many ties of gratitude?*[1]

After issuing further such attacks, only on the day after the Coronation did *The Times* back down, and give the child's illness as the officially accepted reason for the absence of both the Duchess and the Princess. Whatever went on in the family circle (Victoria wept as she watched the procession from Marlborough House), and whatever bitter words were said at Court as a result of the Duchess of Kent's recalcitrance, at least a blind had been put up in public. However, the Duchess of Kent knew that a great deal of popularity-seeking would have to be done to dispel the impressions which the Press's attacks had made on the public mind, which had been retracted by only the most cursory of refutals. Only *The Royal Lady's Magazine*, with a readership miniscule in comparison with those of the major daily newspapers, had been her faithful champion.

Another cause of irritation to King William was the regal state which the Duchess demanded as her daughter's right. In the summer of 1830, while on holiday at Ramsgate, the Duchess had ordered that the Royal Standard should fly over her house at East Cliff. In 1831, Portsmouth garrison fired a gun-salute as the Duchess and her daughter crossed to the Isle of Wight for what was supposedly a private visit to Norris Castle. Gun-salutes were traditionally awarded to members of the royal family only on the occasion of State visits. The whole matter was brought to a head when, in 1832, there began what William was to call the 'royal progresses'—summer journeys throughout England and Wales to introduce the Princess not only to the aristocracy but to 'the people', whose loyalty depended to a great extent on the visibility of their rulers. Everywhere the Duchess and her daughter were greeted by loyal addresses, public celebrations and gun-salutes. A typical example is illustrated by an entry in Princess Victoria's journal:

At ½ past 10 Mamma received an address from the Mayor and Corporation of Beaumaris, and another from the gentlemen in-habitants, and visitors of the town, At ½ past 11 we got into our carriage with my Cousins [two young Mensdorffs] on the box of ours. In passing the Menai-bridge, we received a salute, and on entering the town of Carnarvon, we were met, not only by an immense crowd, who were extremely kind, and pleased, but by the Corporation also, who walked before the carriage, while a salute was firing. We then arrived at the inn, where Mamma received an address, The address being over, we took luncheon, and after that was over, we went to see the ruins of the Castle, which are beautiful, while a salute was fired from the rampart. We then got into the *Emerald*, where we were several times saluted, at the last being nearly becalmed, we were towed by a steam packet, called *Paul Fry*, which saluted us 4 times in the day.[2]

When similar tributes were offered at each stopping-place, and again in the following year, on a tour of the southern counties, the King would tolerate his sister-in-law's presumption no longer. While he himself was earning the country's opprobrium in his political undertakings, especially with respect to the Reform Bill, the Duchess was honouring the age-old Hanoverian tradition of winning support for the heir to the throne, both by throwing in her lot with Parliamentary opposi-

tion and by milching public support. The diarist Greville reports
the inevitable explosion:

> At Court yesterday, and Council for a foolish business. The King
> has been (not unnaturally) disgusted at the Duchess of Kent's
> progresses with her daughter through the kingdom, and amongst
> the rest with her sailings at the Isle of Wight, and the continual
> popping in the shape of salutes to Her Royal Highness. . . . [The
> Council] opened a negotiation with the Duchess of Kent, to induce
> her of her own accord to waive the salutes, and when she went
> to the Isle of Wight to send word that as she was sailing about
> for her own amusement she had rather they did not salute her
> whenever she appeared. The negotiation failed, for the Duchess
> insisted upon her right to be saluted, and would not give it
> up. . . . Conroy (who is a ridiculous fellow, a compound of
> 'Great Hussy' and the Chamberlain of the Princess of Navarre)
> has said "that as her Royal Highness's confidential adviser, he
> could not recommend her to give way on this point".[3]

It took an Order in Council to change the regulations, so that
in future only the King or Queen was to be saluted by guns.
The "continual popping" stopped forthwith, but the "royal
progresses" continued.

Despite the affection which William and Adelaide always
demonstrated to their niece Victoria, her mother held her aloof
from as much as possible of Court life, though on all official
occasions they were in evidence. Memories of Adelaide's kindness to her in the early days of her widowhood could by no
means reconcile the Duchess of Kent to the dangers of expos-
ing Victoria to the possibility of forming attachments to rival
her own influence. The Duchess would keep to her own friends,
and would make her own home entertainments (which were
becoming increasingly elaborate and expensive). She also
kept green her husband's reputation for liberalism by maintaining good relations with Whigs and Radicals of his former
acquaintance—those who were currently clashing with the
King on the problem of Reform. With such provocation, it
cannot be wondered that William IV sometimes retaliated in
kind.

In 1833, the Duchess's Württemburg nephews (sons of her
sister Antoinette) visited England for the London 'season'. They

gratefully accepted invitations to a Court Ball, but the Duchess slighted the Queen by hurrying them away early. As a lady remarked: "The Princess Victoria is sometimes taken to the Opera, and stays till a very late hour, but her Mother took her from the Ball long before it broke up, and on the Queen's saying she hoped at least She would leave her Nephews, She said they had been at a review and were fatigued!!!—Note that they are 6 feet high and very Stout for their age."[4] The Duchess also declined, on the young men's behalf, an invitation to stay some days at Windsor. No excuse can be made for the Duchess's behaviour. The incident can only serve to illustrate the relations that existed between Windsor and Kensington, which point to future unpleasant incidents and future examples, on both sides, of determined ill will. Throughout the whole distasteful business, only Queen Adelaide retains an unblemished character, but then she, poor woman, is generally acknowledged to have been angelic—and dull, attributes decidedly unmerited by Victoria, Duchess of Kent. To be sure, after the visit of Ernest and Alexander of Württemburg in 1833, no Coburg relation would again receive so warm a welcome from the Court. The only way to preserve outward peace was to divorce Kensington and Windsor on the personal level—exactly what the Duchess most desired.

There were opportunities in plenty for a reconciliation had the Duchess of Kent ever wished to make one. For example, in 1835, all the members of the royal family gathered at the Chapel Royal of St James's Palace for Princess Victoria's confirmation. The girl came with some trepidation to the rite, awed by the promises she was to make; she had received a letter from her mother that very morning admonishing her to be more friendly and confiding to her, and had resolved to take it to heart: "I went with the firm intention to become a true Christian, to try and comfort my dear Mamma in all her griefs, trials and anxieties, and to become a dutiful and affectionate daughter to her."[5] But family friction marred the solemn moments, as William IV hustled Conroy from the Chapel, ostensibly because the Duchess's retinue was too large, and the Duchess spent the rest of the service glowering at her brother-in-law. There must have been some nasty silences in the party which followed the ceremony.

By now, of course, Victoria herself knew perfectly well what was going on between her elders. When the Duchess planned a trip to the north for September, she begged her mother to cancel it, as it would only upset the King again. Her mother was adamant. They left London on 3rd September. At the end of the month, after the rigours of hours of travel and tedious receptions, during which Victoria was far from well, the Duchess and her daughter came south to Ramsgate, to meet her brother Leopold, King of the Belgians and his second wife, the French Princess Louise. Victoria immediately fell in love with her new aunt and renewed her passionate attachment to her uncle. When they left, early in October, the Princess was feeling ill—which was put down to the emotion of the parting —but the fever which she showed was soon diagnosed as typhoid.

Between 7th and 31st October, Victoria's journal is a blank, though her life was by no means devoid of incident. When the dangers of the illness were over, and the girl was convalescent, the Duchess and Conroy—despite King Leopold's so recent warnings of caution in their treatment of Victoria—had taken advantage of her weakness to put pressure on her (as they had many times before, in less favourable circumstances) for her promise to make Conroy her confidential secretary when she should come to the throne. Through the whole business, Victoria refused to submit, able to rely only on her governess, Lehzen, for comfort and counsel. At one point, she had even to spurn a letter of recommendation of Conroy to the coveted post, which was thrust into her hand for her signature.

No word of the quarrel is committed to the journal of that date—open as it always was to the Duchess's inspection, but one entry, for 5th November, was surely a hint to whoever might be able to read between the lines, of Victoria's dependence on her only champion: "*Dear good* Lehzen takes such care of me, and is so unceasing in her attentions to me, that I shall never be able to repay her sufficiently for it but by my love and gratitude. I never can sufficiently repay her for all she has *borne* and done for me. She is the most *affectionate*, *devoted*, *attached*, and *disinterested* friend I have, and I love her most *dearly*. . . ."⁶ This brief incident, the first concrete evidence of the mother's pressure on the daughter at the instigation of and on behalf of, Conroy, merely presages the feuding that was to come.

This was the year 1835. In a few months, Victoria would be seventeen, with only a year to run before she might reign without her mother's regency. To Conroy, it seemed imperative that contingency arrangements for his and the Duchess's domination of the future Queen should be established.

In January 1836, the party returned to Kensington, and, with the buoyant spirits of youth, Victoria forgot her recent trials in the enjoyment of enlarged and newly-decorated apartments in the Palace. The acquisition of these extra rooms (seventeen in all) had long been a prime object with the Duchess. Since the beginning of William IV's reign, she had made repeated applications to him, occasionally accompanied by various drawn-up plans, for an extension of her quarters; all had been refused. Thus, after all the disputes, the Duchess decided that the only way in which she could spread out in the Palace was to keep the matter a secret from the King, and to have alterations made privately, at her own expense. So the suite of rooms which was 'made over' in the autumn of 1835 was totally kept from William and his administrators at the Board of Works.

For a time the secret was kept. The King had other annoyances to distract him. He was seriously worried by the stream of Coburgs who made their visits to England—Mensdorffs, Württemburgs, Coburg-Kohárys, to say nothing of Leopold, who had not even had the grace to come to London, but had, according to William IV, skulked away from him at Ramsgate. In March 1836, came the sons of Victoria's uncle Ferdinand, Ferdinand and Augustus of Saxe-Coburg-Koháry. The younger Ferdinand was on his way to Portugal to meet his bride, the teenaged Queen Maria da Gloria. Surely some speculation must have been raised in Victoria's mind, as she contemplated her cousin's wedding, as to her own marriage prospects: there had been plans afoot for years, which the

99

King was known to cherish, to marry her to her cousin George of Cambridge, or even to her cousin George of Cumberland, the eventual heir to the throne of Hanover. Thus, when William heard that the very-eligible Ernest and Albert of Saxe-Coburg-Gotha, sons of the Duke, were to arrive within a week of the Kohárys' departure, the King was furious and tried to prevent the visit. He had himself invited the Prince of Orange and his sons to England, with the firm intention of introducing the young men to his niece Victoria, as viable alternatives to an English match. In fact, William could not have made a worse move: the House of Orange was the bitter enemy of the Belgian state which had been wrenched from it, and no friend to King Leopold who ruled the Belgians. This Victoria knew, and though she maintained dignified politeness to the young Dutchmen who danced with her, she described them in the most unflattering terms to her complaisant uncle. The visit of Ernest and Albert, however, was a great success. As usual, Victoria was intoxicated by male company—and she was especially attracted to Albert. . . .

The differences between the King and the Duchess were coming to a crisis. In August 1836, William IV was to let out all his long-pent-up feelings against her. It began when the King invited the Duchess and Victoria to visit Windsor, to stay over the period which comprised his wife's birthday (the 13th), the Duchess's (the 17th) and his own (the 21st). The Duchess replied that she preferred to keep her own birthday at Claremont, ignored the Queen's but said that she would arrive on the 20th, in time for the public celebrations of the King's anniversary. The King said not a word, but when he was in town, on the 20th, to prorogue Parliament, made a sudden visit to Kensington, after the Duchess and her party had already left for Windsor. There, of course, he found the extension of her accommodation. Returning to Windsor, he greeted his niece affectionately, before turning on the Duchess and accusing her of the "unwarrantable liberty" she had taken at Kensington.

But this outburst was nothing in comparison to the public rebuke the King issued the next day. Although the dinner-party on the King's birthday was intended to be a private affair, the guest list had mounted to over a hundred. The Duchess was seated on one side of the King, Victoria opposite. After dinner, when the royal health had been drunk, the King rose to make what was supposed to be a speech of thanks to his guests for their good wishes. What his surprised listeners heard instead was a furious tirade:

> I trust in God that my life may be spared for nine months longer, after which period, in the event of my death, no regency would take place. I should then have the satisfaction of leaving the royal authority to the personal exercise of that young lady. . . , the heiress presumptive of the Crown, and not in the hands of a person now near me, who is surrounded by evil advisers and who is herself incompetent to act with propriety in the station in which she would be placed. I have no hesitation in saying that I have been insulted—grossly and continually insulted—by that person, but I am determined to endure no longer a course of behaviour so disrespectful to me. Amongst many other things I have particularly to complain of the manner in which that young lady has been kept away from my Court; she has been repeatedly kept from my drawing-rooms, at which she ought always to have been present, but I am fully resolved that this shall not happen again. I would have her know that I am King, and I am determined to make my authority respected, and for the future I shall insist and command that the Princess do upon all occasions appear at my Court, as it is her duty to do.[7]

The words with which the King concluded his speech, addressed directly to Victoria, were affectionate and kind, but they did nothing to lighten the atmosphere. The Queen was obviously upset, the Duchess was fuming with rage, while Victoria was openly weeping; the other guests were either gloating at such an outrageous display, or shocked and bewildered. A private admonition was one thing, a public chastisement was another. Had his rank not forbidden the King to make an exhibition of family differences, chivalry to a lady was felt to have claims which would protect the Duchess.

The observer Greville was undoubtedly right in his judgment when he wrote of the episode that the King "has never had the firmness and decision of character a due display of which would have obviated the necessity of such bickerings, and his passion leads him to these indecent exhibitions, which have not the effect of correcting, and cannot fail to have that of exasperating her [the Duchess], and rendering their mutual relations more hopelessly disagreeable".[8] Indeed, far from forcing his sister-in-law to appear at Court with Victoria more often, the birthday speech encouraged her to remain in increased isolation at Kensington.

As Victoria's majority approached, though the King's death seemed imminent, all hopes of a naturally-gained regency for the Duchess waned. The Kensington enclave tightened. Besides the Duchess and Conroy, the partisans included the Duke of Sussex and his sister the Princess Sophia, who both occupied apartments in the Palace. Sussex had lived in ineffectual existence, denied the active careers of his brothers; he had consoled himself for years by participation in family intrigues. Princess Sophia was an invaluable spy at Court, and whole-hearted in her support of the regency plan, being also under the charm of Conroy. She shared his services as Comptroller with the Duchess of Kent, and either gave or was tricked out of large sums of money, which he used to buy an ostentatious estate in Wales. To the conspirators was added, in March 1837, Prince Charles of Leiningen, who had been forewarned by his uncle Leopold against siding with the Conroy regime against Victoria, but whose championship of his mother's cause was to a great extent powered by his own constant need of her financial aid. A minor figure, but one in daily attendance on the machinations, was Lady Flora Hastings, the Duchess's lady-in-waiting since 1832, similarly devoted to Sir John; she was detested by Victoria for her continual slights to Lehzen, encouraged by her superiors. Together, all were ready to make a last attempt to cower or cajole the Princess Victoria into acquiescence to their schemes before she slipped through their fingers.

Their chance came on 19th May, the day before Victoria's eighteenth birthday. The King sent Lord Conyngham to Kensington with a letter for Victoria, in which he offered her an income of £10,000 which she should control herself. Conyngham had orders to give the letter only to the Princess herself, and was embarrassed at finding her in the company of her mother and Conroy when he was shown into her presence. The Duchess put out her hand to take the letter, and he drew back. He explained his charge to deliver it to her daughter, and the girl was allowed to take the letter from him.

When Conynham had gone, Victoria was also allowed to read her letter, but then the others fell on it. The independent allowance was bad enough, but the Duchess was furious when she found that a Crown servant was to be put to administer the money, and that her daughter was to be allowed to choose her own ladies. Conroy too was angry, for he knew that there would be no chance of a place in Victoria's service for his own daughters if the Princess had a say in the matter.

The next morning, Victoria was presented with a pre-written letter to the King, in which she accepted the money only with the proviso that her mother should control it. She refused to sign, and begged to consult the Prime Minister, Lord Melbourne —was refused, then signed unwillingly. That very day, she and Lehzen wrote secretly a statement that Victoria had not herself replied to the King's offer, and that she had not truly approved the contents of the letter she had signed. It was put into safe-keeping against the day on which it might be needed to prove her non-involvement in her mother's schemes.

Victoria's birthday was celebrated with public cheerfulness by all concerned, despite the undercurrents of resentment. Loyal addresses were presented to the Princess, and one man who came in a deputation to Kensington on this errand described the scene:

What struck me most was the hopefulness that pervaded the assembled well-wishers. The breath of Spring was in the air outside; the breath of a moral and political Spring, of renovation and resurrection, buoyed us up within . . . we were all happy that day as the birds on the branches. The Duchess was an exception. She was, we thought, anxious and harassed, but was finely dressed, and had a fine neck to show, though rather a stout one. If there was anything the matter with her hair, a magnificent plumed hat hid it. The Princess stood beside her, also in evening dress and hat. She was pretty, but her face, somehow, was not quite satisfactory. I cannot tell at this distance of time what was the matter with it; but I was less taken with her than with her mother. . . . The mother did not strike us as a woman of race or breeding, only as an excellent, rather handsome person, and a lady that would make a good mother-in-law. . . . The Princess was as cool as she ever showed herself since . . . she was quite grown up, but no height. The addresses were read to *her*, and were answered by her mother, who read with a German accent, but otherwise well.[9]

The private brow-beatings continued. The Prime Minister had been informed of the terms of the Princess's accepting the King's money (which amounted, in William's eyes, to a refusal of it), and, knowing nothing of Kensington Palace's internal politics, saw the collision in terms of Parliamentary politics; the Tories might make capital out of the affair if it became common knowledge. When Melbourne offered the Duchess a new settlement, £6,000 for herself and £4,000 for Victoria, she refused.

Another person who was informed of the exchange, and who saw a copy of the letter which Victoria had signed, was King Leopold, her distant but ever-watchful mentor. Shrewd enough to weigh up the garbled accounts he received from the mother and daughter, from his nephew and from Lehzen, Leopold wrote to his niece on 25th May: "My dearest Child,—You have had some battles and difficulties of which I am completely in the dark. . . . Two things seem necessary; not to be fettered by any establishment other than will be *comfortable to you*, and then to avoid any breach with your mother. . . . Be steady, my good child, and not put out by anything; as long as I live *you will not want a faithful friend and supporter*. . . ."[10] Leopold had been alerted to the situation at Kensington a month previously by his nephew Leiningen, who claimed (on Conroy's priming) that Victoria really *needed* a regency, being too immature to cope with the task of ruling without help. Leopold was inclined to agree with him there, but was more anxious that Victoria should have the reins of power nominally in her hands, and should continue to rely on him, to the exclusion of her mother and Conroy. If the Duchess was awarded a new regency at the eleventh hour, Leopold now stood no chance of making his influence felt. Accordingly, the King of the Belgians sent over one whom all parties had known for years, and would trust to soothe the differences, but who was totally pledged to his, Leopold's, interests: this was Edward Stockmar, the Coburg's 'trouble-shooter', who had been in the family service since the early years of the century. He had held Princess Charlotte's hands in her death-throes; he had supervised the Duke of Kent's making of his Will; he had furthered Leopold's interest on the Continent when the crown of Belgium was in the offing; he knew all the parties concerned in the Kensington intrigue, and had long since made memoranda on the situation on every visit to England that he made.

Stockmar found the Princess still refusing to commit herself to any of the plans for an extended period of minority, or for Conroy to take a post about her; she withstood the combined pressure of her mother, Sir John and now her half-brother with a firmness and decision remarkable in one of her age (though Lehzen's support and prompting should not be underestimated). With the strong-minded and resolute Stockmar at her side, she grew even bolder, refusing to read any note which came from her brother Charles, or to submit to the tearful blandishments in any missive from her mother. The Duchess had always found it difficult to talk to her daughter at moments of stress, and her resorting to note-writing was always a sign that she could not trust herself to speak calmly, or to retain her still imperfect command of English.

Early in June, news of the King's death was expected daily. But still there were a few tricks up Conroy's sleeve. He persuaded the Duchess of Kent to write to Melbourne, telling him that it was her daughter's wish that his government should introduce a new Regency Bill into Parliament. Stockmar found out what was happening, denounced Conroy to Melbourne and explained the real situation, The Prime Minister was "struck all of a heap"[11] when he heard what had been going on, and promised to have nothing more to do with the matter. Foiled again, Kensington called in Lord Liverpool. First he saw Conroy who told him that Victoria was mentally unstable and in need of a private secretary who, by long experience of her deficiencies, could guide her—namely himself. Then Liverpool saw Victoria herself—alone—and she quickly disabused him of any false notions; she would never consent, she said, to employ Sir John Conroy in any capacity, and would place herself in Melbourne's hands when she came to the throne. She showed him a letter she had written, with Lehzen as a witness, annulling any promise she might be forced to make. Liverpool recognized her determination and respected her for it. He left immediately.

Victoria was confined to her room and, according to Greville, "Conroy urged the Duchess to . . . keep her under duress till she had extorted this engagement from her; but the spirit of the daughter and the timidity of the mother prevented this plot taking effect."[12] (Greville's informant was Lord Melbourne, in later years, when the Prime Minister had heard all the ins and outs from Victoria herself.) The Duchess was weakening; both she and her son had taken fright at what might happen should Victoria's reign begin without Conroy's ascendancy having been guaranteed; she wrote to Victoria warning her not to have too much confidence in herself; she would find, said the Duchess, that ruling England was anything but easy: "You are still very young and all your success so far has been due to your *Mother's* reputation. Do not be *too sanguine* in *your* own *talents* and understanding."[13] But such a reminder was too late; by then, Victoria knew her own power, and her own potential.

That letter was written on 13th June. On the 20th, at about two in the morning, William IV died. Three hours later, the news reached Kensington. Howley, Archbishop of Canterbury, Conyngham, the Lord Chamberlain, and Sir Henry Halford, the King's doctor, arrived. The Duchess was woken and went downstairs to receive them. At first she refused to wake her daughter, but then, when asked to rouse 'the Queen", she submitted. In her journal, Victoria was to write: "I was awoke at 6 o'clock by Mamma. . . ."[14] In her own diary, the Duchess qualified that statement with the words "with a kiss".[15]

NOTES TO CHAPTER SEVEN

1   *The Times*, 7.9.31.
2   Esher (ed.), *Girlhood of Queen Victoria*, volume i, pp. 45–6: 9.8.32.
3   Reeve (ed.), *Greville Memoirs*, volume i, part iii, p. 3: 4.7.33.
4   Egerton Castle (ed.), *Jerningham Papers*, volume ii, pp. 367–8.
5   Esher (ed.), *op. cit.*, volume i, pp. 124–6: 30.7.35.
6   *Ibid.*, volume i, p. 138: 5.11.35.
7   Reeve (ed.), *op. cit.*, volume i, part iii, pp. 366–9.
8   *Ibid.*
9   Potter, Founder of the Cobden Club: Creston, *Youthful Queen Victoria*, pp. 226–7.
10 Leopold, King of the Belgians, to Princess Victoria, 25.5.37: Benson and Esher (ed.), *Letters of Queen Victoria*, volume i, pp. 67–8.
11 Strachey and Fulford (ed.), *Greville Memoirs*, volume vii, p. 70: 30.10.54.
12 *Ibid.*, volume iv, pp. 44–5: 25.3.38.
13 Victoria, Duchess of Kent, to Princess Victoria, 13.6.37: RA M7/52: Longford, *Victoria R.I.*, p. 73.
14 Esher (ed.), *op. cit.*, volume i, pp. 195–6: 20.6.37.
15 Duchess of Kent's diary, 20.6.37: RA Z 294: Longford, *op. cit.*, p. 75.

CHAPTER EIGHT

The Queen's Mother

What did Britain know of her eighteen-year-old Queen when the news of her accession rippled through the kingdom in June 1837? Unlike her two predecessors, her uncles George IV and William IV, Victoria had played not the slightest part in national affairs before her accession. She had been seen only rarely—and then silently—at Court, only briefly in the country houses of the great aristocrats. 'The people' had observed her on meteoric summer journeys through the provinces—and as far north as York, a rare feat for a member of the royal family—but only some few of them had heard her silver-voiced replies to their speeches of welcome. Her mother was right when she claimed that any popularity Victoria had in the country had been built up by her own efforts.

The Queen's character was as yet a mystery to her subjects. The perceptive Greville himself, though no stranger to royal circles, wrote, a few days before the accession:

What renders speculation so easy, and events so uncertain, is the absolute ignorance of everybody, without exception, of the character, disposition, and capacity of the Princess. She has been kept in such jealous seclusion by her Mother (never having slept out of her bedroom, nor been alone with anybody but herself and Baroness Lehzen), that not one of her acquaintances, none of the Attendants at Kensington, not even the Duchess of Northumberland, her [State] governess, have any idea what She is, or what She promises to be. It is therefore no difficult matter to form and utter conjectures, which nobody can contradict or

gainsay but by other conjectures equally uncertain and falla-
cious.[1]

But the first day of Victoria's reign left the few people who
met her in no doubt as to her capabilities, her resolution and
the policies which she had already secretly formulated as to
her future dealings with those who had been closest to her all
her life.

When Victoria hastened downstairs to meet the gentlemen
who were to announce to her the news of her uncle's death,
her mother followed close behind, but when she entered the
sitting-room in which they had been waiting, she was alone.
After that interview, she dressed quickly and received Stockmar
during breakfast. He probably reminded her of the devotion
and steadfast encouragement of her uncle Leopold, for it was
to him that the Queen wrote first, at 8.30. While she was
occupied in informing her half-sister Feodora of the news,
Victoria received a note from Lord Melbourne, the Prime
Minister, who came to her at nine o'clock, and whom she saw
"in my room, and *of course quite alone*, as I shall *always* do
all my Ministers".[2] She repeated that assertion with regard to
the Council meeting which she attended at 11.30: "I went in
of course quite alone. . . ."[3] Throughout the journal entry for
that day, that word 'alone' is repeated so often—she saw
Ministers of State and the Archbishop of Canterbury 'alone',
she dined 'alone': unaccustomed pleasures on that day of
unmitigated excitement on which Victoria began her new life.

And throughout the day, Victoria was wonderfully polite to
her mother, but would not allow her the fatigue of joining
her in her work—the very business that the Duchess most
desired. It is of paramount significance that, on that first day,
with cares of a new sort crowding in, Sir John Conroy was
not forgotten by the Duchess. After the Council, Stockmar
accosted Melbourne with the news that Conroy had already
pestered him for good 'terms' for his—as he saw it, inevitable
—retirement from the Duchess's service: a pension of £3,000
a year, the Grand Cross of the Bath, a peerage and a seat on
the Privy Council. Melbourne was astounded at the man's
'impudence'. Repeatedly, the Duchess sent notes to her

daughter, even in the midst of the Queen's first consideration of her new duties, and received no satisfaction. By the last, the Duchess had become sarcastic: "Lord Melbourne will find out very quickly that you are not gracious to Sir John...."[4]

Again, the Duchess had made a mistake. Now was not the time to remind her daughter of the recent quarrels—not now, at a time at which the emotion of the hour might have induced Victoria into making a reconciliation with her mother. She and Conroy should have tried to bide their time. As it was, the last lines of the Queen's diary for her accession day read: "Went down and said good night to Mamma &c. My dear Lehzen will ALWAYS remain with me as my friend...."[5] And for the first time since her infancy, Victoria did not sleep in her mother's bed. In the span of one day, the chains of a lifetime had been broken.

Although the calm self-possession and resolution of the teen-aged Queen came as a surprise to those who met her for the first time at her accession, it is easily explained, in retrospect, with the facts.

If Victoria had obediently followed the 'Kensington system' of total dependence on her mother and respect for Conroy, her childhood and young womanhood would probably have been unclouded. King Leopold could perhaps have been kept at bay, and Lehzen relegated strictly to her role of governess. Instead, from about the age of twelve, she had been fully aware of the self-interest which governed her elders, and while maintaining outward politeness for the most part, was inwardly rebellious much of the time. Lehzen had taught her this deviousness, so that while the Duchess of Kent was chiding her daughter for her admiration of 'simplicity' of character, that same child was herself carrying out a complicated routine of deception. The obstinacy which Victoria maintained in refusing to be cowed by Conroy and her mother, though it came as a surprise to them, was natural not only from her stolid Hanoverian heredity but from the years of bottled-up resentment.

In fact, Victoria's character was exceedingly complex. Once she had made up her mind, she could be affectionate and loyal or totally antipathetic. She could lean on Lehzen and listen with docility to her uncle Leopold, but then neither of them tried to cross her will in anything important. She could romp like a child, and then turn on the icy stare which said so plainly: "We are not amused." But she was insecure: her idolatry of Lehzen showed that, as did the emergence of Melbourne as a father-figure in the first days of her reign. She was also emotionally unstable, knowing the depths of depression in alternation with the heights of merriment. But all Victoria's paradoxes and contradictions of character added up to one thing: she would be Queen in her own way; Lehzen would never influence her politics and Melbourne would never rule her personal plans. Her discarding of the two faithful devotees when Albert, her husband, displaced them in her affections proves their merely temporary hold. It was only when Victoria came to maturity that she allowed unrestricted domination of her to fall to another person, and that not until after many struggles to maintain the independence that she had won in so fierce a battle.

The few days following immediately upon the accession saw repeated assertions of Victoria's independence. On the 21st, she drove to St James's to hear the proclamation of her reign, and the Duchess went with her, but at the ceremony, it was noted, the Duchess was "not prominent". On that occasion, the Queen was hailed as 'Alexandrina Victoria', both her baptismal names; it was only the next day that it was decided that she was to be called 'Victoria' officially—a wry twist of fate which must have reminded the elder Victoria of that June christening in 1819.

As the first weeks of the new reign passed, the Duchess of Kent found herself being imperceptibly ousted from her daughter's daily routine. A month after the accession, the move from Kensington to Buckingham Palace was effected. Here it was even more noticeable·that Victoria had little desire to share her time with her mother, whose rooms were as far away from the Queen's apartments as possible, though in Victoria's bedroom wall a hole had opened up access to Lehzen's chamber.

Indiscreetly, the Duchess was forthcoming to the inquisitive Princess Lieven on the situation between her daughter and herself, so that her confidante could soon inform the whole of Europe that the Duchess of Kent felt

> overwhelmed with vexation and disappointment. Her daughter behaves to her with kindness and attention, but has rendered herself quite independent of the Duchess, who painfully feels her own insignificance. The almost contemptuous way in which Conroy has been dismissed must be a bitter mortification to her, and all things considered is scarcely decent. He has been amply rewarded by a pension of 3,000 a year, but the contrast between this pecuniary munificence and his personal exclusion from Court has a remarkable and rather mysterious appearance [in fact, it seemed to *prove* to courtiers that the Queen believed Conroy to be her mother's lover]. The Duchess said to Madame de Lieven, *"qu'il n'y avait plus d'avenir pour elle, qu'elle n'était plus rien"*; that for eighteen years this child had been the sole object of her life, of all her thoughts and hopes, and now She was taken from her, and there was an end of all for which she had lived heretofore. Madame de Lieven said that she ought to be the happiest of human beings, to see the elevation of this child, her prodigious success, and the praise and admiration of which she was universally the object; that it was a triumph and a glory which ought to be sufficient for her—to which she only shook her head with a melancholy smile, and gave her to understand that all this would not do, and that the accomplishment of her wishes had only made her to the last degree unhappy. King William is revenged, he little anticipated how or by what instrumentality, and if his ghost is an ill-natured and vindictive shade, it may rejoice in this bitter disappointment of his enemy.[6]

If King William could indeed enjoy his revenge on the Duchess, he could also rejoice in the Queen's deference to his Adelaide, and in her generosity to his Fitzclarence children, who were continued in their posts and who received handsome pensions.

In the place which Conroy must coveted—that of confidential adviser to the Queen—stood a far more worthy mentor, the Prime Minister, Lord Melbourne. From the turmoils of the last days preceding her reign, Melbourne had emerged as an honest and dependable man, in Victoria's eyes. When she came to the throne, she was ready to lean on him and to use his wide

"A scene in the new farce called 'The Rivals', or a visit to the Heir Presumptive"—the "Rival Pregnancies" cartoon. The couples are, from left to right, the Clarences, the Cambridges, the Kents and the Cumberlands, with the Duchess of York in the foreground, right (reproduced by courtesy of the British Museum)

(*left*) Louise, Baroness Lehzen, governess to Princess Victoria—a miniature by Koepke (reproduced by gracious permission of H.M. The Queen); (*right*) Princess Feodora in 1828, by Collen (reproduced by gracious permission of H.M. The Queen)

(*left*) Charles, Prince of Leiningen, from a portrait by Sir David Wilkie (reproduced by courtesy of the Mansell Collection); (*right*) Leopold I, King of the Belgians, by F. Winterhalter (reproduced by courtesy of the Mansell Collection)

knowledge of contemporary politics, foreign affairs and world history to supplement her own mediocre store. But after a time, Victoria found more in Melbourne than a mere teacher: he became the most interesting and absorbing person in her life—far more fascinating than Lehzen, if not so doting. Melbourne's unhappy past—his disastrous marriage to Lady Caroline Lamb, the recent death of his only son—was detailed to the Queen by gossiping ladies, and may have explained to her, as it does to later researchers, her charms for him. Though well supplied with feminine company of the mature, sophisticated variety, Melbourne found uniquely in Victoria a reminder of his once innocent bride, and the child whose society he had never shared. For Victoria, he was the father-figure which Conroy had failed to supply (how immense could his influence have been if he had!) and the link with the worldlings from whom she had always been protected. Melbourne knew exactly what would please the girl—admiration for the ubiquitous Lehzen, and respect for King Leopold.

Leopold himself now took second place to Melbourne in Victoria's affections, and his advice was weighed carefully against that of the Prime Minister. In the first flush of pride at owning her own home, Victoria invited her uncle to visit her, and he came in August—eager to find out what place in the scheme of things his niece, now so unrecognizably her own mistress, would allocate to him. The King of the Belgians soon found out that while he could safely instruct his niece Victoria on historical precedent and the general demeanour of a monarch, the Queen of England would retain for Melbourne the prerogative of specific advice on policy.

However, on one point, Leopold was gratifyingly useful: he talked to the Duchess of Kent about her relationship with her daughter—which was now rapidly deteriorating into demanding notes on one side, and brief, curt replies on the other. The Queen would frequently answer her mother's petitions to see her during the day with the one word, "Busy". But after Leopold's visit, Princess Lieven was informed that the Duchess "no longer appears disgruntled as she used to do, that she is in better spirits, and that she even intends to cast off her gentleman, which would be a wise step for her as well as for everyone else, for they say he bullies her incessantly".[7]

The problem of Conroy was to colour the whole year after Victoria came to the throne. The Queen informed him in a frosty interview that the pension he had asked for would be his, but that the 'red riband' and the peerage (even of the Irish variety) were in the hands of her ministers, and she could promise nothing. Thus Conroy felt it unnecessary to fulfil his part of the bargain, his resignation. But if Victoria could not oust him by agreement, she could at least make his position intolerable. She refused to allow Sir John to be of her party at a banquet at the Guildhall on 9th November 1837, as a definitely intended slight. The Duchess wrote pitifully to the Queen: "Really dearest Angel we have made too much of this affair.... I have the greatest regard for Sir John. I cannot forget what he has done for me and for you! although he had the misfortune to displease you!"[8]

Throughout 1837 and 1838, there were schemes always in hand to persuade or frighten Conroy into resigning; none succeeded. Those who saw the Duchess yawning over her whist-game every evening in the Queen's drawing-room might realize that Victoria had no affection for her mother, but they could scarcely realize the terrible undercurrents of jealousy and resentment between them. The Duchess not only envied Lehzen her share in the Queen's confidence, but now came to regard Lord Melbourne as a rival. Whenever she could, she delayed her daughter in her company, so as to keep the Prime Minister waiting—reliance on the Queen's perfect politeness to her in public was her only weapon. But she felt deeply the "ingratitude" of her daughter. It was surely no coincidence that she gave Victoria a copy of *King Lear* for her nineteenth birthday.

Three incidents occurring between January and September 1839 opened still further the rift between the Queen and her mother. They were the tragic death of Lady Flora Hastings, the Duchess's lady-in-waiting, after months of scandal during which the Queen was the foremost among her persecutors; the 'Bed-chamber Plot', which was linked tenuously with the Lady Flora affair, and which rocked and then shattered the short-lived first ministry of Robert Peel; and the final confrontation on the dismissal of Conroy.

Lady Flora had been the Duchess's lady-in-waiting since 1832, when she was in her mid-twenties. She was also a poet of no little distinction. The young Victoria had always disliked her, as being a partisan in the Conroy regime, an unwelcome third in many a thwarted *tête-à-tête* with Lehzen and also the persistent persecutor, by sneers and innuendo, of the favoured governess. Now, the Queen's ladies, who came into contact with her daily, followed their mistress's lead: they shunned Lady Flora, averring that she was to be seen continually in the company of Conroy, who was universally detested. Lady Flora was good-looking and elegant, and, in 1839, at the age of thirty-two, still unmarried; why so, if she did not harbour a secret passion for a married man?

In January, the Queen's sharp eyes noted the increased bulk of Lady Flora's figure, despite her voluminous skirts; Victoria and Lehzen agreed that it seemed as if Lady Flora were pregnant. The seniors among the Queen's ladies, too, were suspicious, which was enough to convince Victoria that Lady Flora was indeed "with child"!! . . . the cause of all this is the monster and demon incarnate",[9] Conroy. Everyone remembered that Lady Flora had returned from a Christmas holiday at home in Scotland with Conroy as her 'protector' on the journey—unchaperoned. Though she was having medical treatment for a bowel disturbance and abdominal pains of which she believed the swelling to be a symptom, Lady Flora's doctor admitted that his diagnosis—or rather the conclusion he had drawn from it—might be faulty, and that she could be pregnant. He was charged to suggest to his patient that she must be secretly married. With indignation, she scorned the imputation. Privately, Lady Flora was forbidden to appear before the Queen until she could prove her innocence, or legalize her presumed state.

It was only on 16th February that the Duchess was told. She was 'horror-struck'. On hearing that Lady Flora had been requested to undergo a full internal examination (such an ordeal to delicate female sensibilities), she was revolted. As Lady Flora herself later wrote: "She shrunk with horror from the idea of my submitting to the test demanded, but I urged her, for my sake, and for that of my family, and for her own, for I felt it right towards her to allow me to meet the charge in the manner most convincingly, and instantly to refute it. I was strong in innocence and I felt my courage equal to any endurance."[10] But the test settled nothing: the doctors awarded her a certificate attesting her virginity, but virtually nullified its worth by dredging up from their memory cases of pregnancy in women still technically virgins.

The matter was not, of course, allowed to rest, but all the blame for its continuation did not lie with Lady Flora's antagonists. The unpleasant publicity which ensued was due mainly to the interference of Lady Flora's brother, the Marquess of Hastings, to whom she had recounted the whole episode. He charged the two senior ladies of the Queen, Ladies Tavistock and Portman, with scandal-mongering, and ascribed the origins of the gossip to "the *baneful influence* which surrounds the throne, and poisons and deadens all the best feelings and dictates of human nature"[11]—Lehzen.

Both Melbourne and the Duke of Wellington had been dragged into the arena—the latter by the Duchess of Kent, who regarded the old soldier as her own particular champion. She exerted herself beyond all reasonable limits for her protégée (surely some proof that she had not herself been Conroy's mistress, for she could not have trusted Lady Flora's protestations of innocence had there been any element of jealousy involved). When an article appeared in the Press, on 24th March, by a Mr Hamilton Fitzgerald, an uncle of Lady Flora Hastings, castigating the supposed culprits of the rumours, the Duchess was the only person in the royal circle to be held blameless. Fitzgerald quoted a letter he had received from his niece:

The Duchess was perfect. A mother could not have been kinder, and she took up the insult as a personal one, directed as it was at a person attached to her service, and devoted to her. She directly dismissed Sir James Clark [the Court doctor] and refused to see Lady Portman, and would neither re-appear nor suffer me re-appear at the Queen's table for many days. She has crowned her goodness by a most beautiful letter she has written to poor mamma, whom the accounts, kept from her while there was a hope that matters might not become public, would reach today. . . . The Duchess has stood by me gallantly, and I love her better than ever. She is the most generous-souled woman possible, and such a heart! This business had made her very ill.[12]

No one but the Queen laid any blame on the Duchess throughout the whole sad affair.

But Lady Flora's tribulations were not merely a social scandal; they reverberated in the political sphere as well. The Queen was a staunch Whig, thoroughly satisfied with Lord Melbourne's ministry, but Parliament was not so certain, with Tory members and Radicals on the increase, and the Whigs split among themselves. On 22 March, the Government had been defeated by five votes in the Lords; by the beginning of May, the Jamaica Bill promised further defeats. The Whigs could so easily be swept away, and the Queen's long-hated Tories imposed on her as her new Government. On 7th May, she sobbed as Lord John Russell told her that Melbourne must go.

Now began a true battle-royal, as the incoming Premier, Peel, told Victoria that she must give up the Whig ladies of her household (which was predominantly of that party) to be replaced by wives and daughters of the Tories. This is where the connection with Lady Flora came in, for the Whig Ladies Tavistock and Portman, who had been so abused by the Press for their part against her, would be the first to go. But the Queen proved recalcitrant. Her beloved Melbourne *must* be dismissed, she could understand that—but her ladies, never! She claimed, with probable justification, that she never discussed politics with her ladies, but with the Lady Flora issue now becoming a matter of party divisions (her brother was a Tory), politics and personal opinion seemed indivisible.

On the night of 10th May, Melbourne read through the exchange of letters between the Queen and Peel at an emergency meeting of his party. Forgetting past differences, they backed him to a man. This was the reason that the episode came to be known as the 'Bedchamber Plot', for the Tories saw

Melbourne's use of the Queen's attachment to the Ladies of the Bedchamber as a factor paramount in the defeat of Peel. The day after the meeting, Peel was forced to resign his office of Prime Minister, which he had held so briefly. The crisis had lasted less than a week. Melbourne was back in power—and in the Palace. The Queen was content.

Since the outbreak of the scandal, Sir John Conroy had been lying low. His only part had been to prosecute *The Times* for the calumnies against him which it had published; he was to have the satisfaction of seeing the editor gaoled for three months. As well as having an enemy in the Queen, Conroy now alienated the Duchess's German children and her Coburg relations: when they visited her and the Queen, they found him insolently continuing to use his privilege of access to the private sitting-rooms, even when they were *en famille*. They informed Wellington of the state of affairs and warned the Duchess to do nothing without his advice. Throughout May, discussions and negotiations were going on between Conroy and his associates to find a way of ending the deadlock between the Queen and her mother, of which he was undoubtedly the prime cause. John Abercromby, Lord Dunfermline, wrote to him on 25th May:

You cannot be ignorant that it is everywhere boldly asserted, that your remaining in the family of the Duchess of Kent, is the main cause and even the sole cause of that disunion which is to be deplored. . . . If your withdrawal leads to cordial union between Her Majesty and her mother, you will, I am sure, rejoice in the happy results. If it fails to produce that effect, you will have the satisfaction of proving that what has been so generally asserted is untrue, and you will also have the consciousness of having taken that course, which all reasonable men most approve.[18]

On 1st June, Conroy wrote the Duchess a formal letter of resignation. Immediately on receiving it, she sent for Wellington, and showed him both Conroy's letter and Dunfermline's which was now in her possession. Wellington added his voice to those urging her to accept the offer. He added:

That under these Circumstances I would recommend to H.R.H. to take Her Station in the Palace as if nothing had happened.

To do everything which her own Affection for Her Daughter the Queen and Her good sense, would suggest, to conciliate to Herself the Queen and all Her Family and Court; and to choose for herself afterwards whether it was expedient that she should write to H.M. upon the sacrifice which she made in receiving the Resignation of Her Servant. I said that it appeared to me most desirable that she should not avert to such sacrifices.[14]

The Duchess of Kent was duly grateful to the Duke of Wellington, and wrote to him on 3rd June:

My dear Duke

It is only now, I turn in my mind all you said to me, I see the greatness of your views for the Queen's honour and happiness, and feel to the *Bottom* of *my heart* your *goodness* to me.

I will do all you desire, but my mind is so *worked* I fear I must wait a day before I am *able* to speak to Lord Melbourne. Would to God that my dear Child could speak to you, I see and feel your *devotion* to *Her* and to your *Country*; I do appreciate your conduct at this Crisis; May your precious life be spared. As I found it necessary to see you, because I doubted Sir John Conroy saying a word for himself, I feel how right I was to see you, as we did justice to that faithful Man's deserts, and I had also the benefit of all the advice you gave me, in consequence on every point I touched on.

I shall write to Sir John Conroy your approbation, would you do so *yourself* it would be a great support, I am sure, to His feelings, for he has behaved nobly by me, but in doing so, I have lost the most *devoted* of followers and the most *faithful* of friends.

Believe me with real regard and esteem, my dear Duke,

Your very grateful and sincere friend

Victoria[15]

On the 10th, the Duchess wrote to Conroy himself. At first her phrasing is circumspect, praising his service to herself and her late husband, but by the last page it has become querulous and pathetic:

. . . for twenty years I have availed myself of your assistance, to the fullest extent and have profited from your ability, exertions and zeal. You have possessed my *entire* confidence. I gave it you *freely*—because I knew that it was reposed in one who would not abuse it.—I shall *always feel, how much I owe,* to your friendship; and shall *ever retain* the most unshaken esteem of your character.[16]

Inevitably, Princess Lieven was one of the first to be ferreting for the inside story of the apparently voluntary resignation. She reported to a friend that she had seen Sir John, who had told her that

. . . he blamed Leopold *for everything* absolutely. He says that from the year '35 onwards he plotted with the governess to deprive the mother of all influence over her daughter, in order that his influence alone should prevail. Only the first part of the plan succeeded. It was the governess who profited, and not Leopold. He speaks with great respect of the Queen, and says that he is attached to her because she is the daughter of the Duke of Kent. He does not think that the mother and daughter will ever be able to agree.[17]

Of course, Conroy was right in ascribing the Queen's antipathy to him to the years before her succession, but the immediate cause of his resignation was the scandal of 1839. Not only his suspected paternity of Lady Flora's supposed child, but his influence on the Duchess throughout the affair, had had the most harmful effect in further alienating the Duchess from the Queen.

Though Conroy was now no longer under her roof to trouble Victoria, and though she showed signs of relief that her mother was now out of his power, the Queen was not permitted to forget her old enemy's existence. Five years later, he was still pestering her ministers on the matter of the Irish peerage that he believed had been promised him. He had kept transcripts of all the letters he had sent and received which referred to the peerage, and which he considered proved his entitlement. When the peerage was withheld for so many years that it would surely never materialize, Conroy began to bemoan his hard treatment at the Queen's hands. All his papers on the subject were retained by his children after his death, at his own request, lest any malice should raise the matter against him. These papers are now housed in the Library of Balliol College, Oxford, together with other family papers which include affectionate letters from the Duchess of Kent to Conroy's children. At his death, however, she demanded the return of all letters she had written to Sir John, and those which her brother Leopold and her son had sent him. There is thus little left among the papers to throw light on the relationship between the Duchess and the former Comptroller of her household and controller of her life —though everything there has been sifted many times by the multifarious biographies of Queen Victoria. There is not one word to clarify his schemes before Victoria's accession or to amplify common knowledge of his part in the Lady Flora Hastings scandal.

That month of June 1839 in which Conroy left her employment, was a bad time for the Duchess. Lady Flora's illness, which had shown some signs of abating in the past weeks, was renewed. When rumours were put about that Lady Flora was dying, the Queen softened her attitude, even offering to visit her. On 27th June they met. Victoria was shocked and dismayed by her gaunt appearance, and by the pathetic, rebuking way in which Lady Flora had received her. On 4th July came the news that Lady Flora Hastings had died. A post-mortem explained why her expected child had not been born: she had never been pregnant; she had been suffering from a tumour of the liver which had caused the swelling of her body.

Inevitably, there was more publicity. In September, Lord Hastings published the correspondence he had conducted with Melbourne and others to win their support to clear his sister's name. He had thought that this revelation might blacken the Prime Minister's name and, as a Tory still burdened with a Whig Government, cared little how much damage he did. But Lord Hastings was to be disappointed. At last, the public had tired of the stale quarrel. The scandal was over. It had not only blighted the last months of Lady Flora Hastings's life, at a time at which she might have expected the deepest consideration, but had also ended the first phase of the Queen's popularity. (She was even hissed by titled ladies at the Races.) The whole affair had depressed Victoria completely; the first exhilarating days of her reign were over; she was unwell, listless and irritable then over-excited and noisy—her emotional balance was disturbed. She feared the future and shuddered at the past.

But for the Duchess of Kent, the worst was over. There was

a temporary lull in the storm. Though the Queen still privately intimated that she would prefer that her mother move out of Buckingham Palace, she wrote her a conciliatory letter, commending the "sacrifice" that she had made on her behalf in allowing Conroy to go. The Duchess of Kent took Wellington's advice that she should behave normally to her daughter, and that she should conciliate those whom she had come to hate, Lehzen and Melbourne, who had not only won her daughter's whole affections but who had acted so badly to Lady Flora. When the Duchess complained that Melbourne took up too much of Victoria's time, the Duke of Wellington only laughed at her—had he been Prime Minister, he said, he would have taken up residence in the Palace so as to be always with the Queen.

According to Greville, the Duchess asked Wellington, " '. . . what must I do if She [Victoria] asks me to shake hands with Letzen [sic]?'—'Do? Why, take her in your arms and kiss her.' Here the Duchess burst out laughing, in which the Duke joined, when he said, 'I don't mean you are to take Letzen in your arms and kiss her, but the Queen'."[18] And so all was amicably agreed, and the Duchess of Kent determined to regain her daughter's love and respect by strenuous exertions in conciliation.

Victoria's mind was very much on marriage that year. At the height of the Lady Flora affair, and with the Bedchamber Plot raging around her, the Queen could still enjoy a romantic interlude with the visiting Tsarevitch Alexander. She confessed to her journal that she was a little in love with him. With the division of her time between the elderly Lehzen and the equally mature Melbourne, she still craved the company of young people, and any favours she distributed to the young men of her Court were watched with apprehension by her advisers.

But though her thoughts were often on marriage, Victoria, in her mood of depression, was temporarily prejudiced against it. She was afraid that she would lose her independence; that by seeking a new sort of happiness, she would be bringing upon herself only a new sort of misery. She felt safe with Lehzen and Melbourne, and feared new relationships; but she still yearned for a closer, more equal companion. It was a contradiction within her mind that she found difficult to resolve.

However, her uncle Leopold still clung to his long-held ambition to marry her to her cousin Albert, and was now urging her to meet him once more and make up her mind. The young man had been groomed for the position; his education had been undertaken with the young Victoria consulted at every step. When she had met Albert in 1836, and found that he preferred study and family gatherings to the social life which would be expected of her husband, the young Victoria had suggested that he be rather more polished by association with 'society people' of the Continent, and her advice was taken. A lot of thought and planning, as well as obedience on Albert's part, had gone into providing a perfect match for the Queen of England.

Leopold's scheme was not to be thwarted by the Queen's being out of temper. He prepared the way for his nephew by means of his brother Ferdinand, who brought his three younger children and their cousin Alexander Mensdorff-Pouilly to England in September 1839. They found the Queen ready for some fun, after her dreary summer. But if the Coburg-Koharys caught Victoria's fancy, cousin Mensdorff, a serious, shy young soldier, was even more attractive. The group of them would play games in the evenings, chattering in German, while poor Melbourne—by now used to being the centre of attention in the Queen's drawing-room—sat apart, not understanding the foreign conversation. When the holiday came to an end, Victoria accompanied her guests to the waiting ship, sobbing openly at the wrench of parting. Inevitably, the Duchess of Kent had been brought to the fore during her brother's stay, and had for a time enjoyed a period of harmony with her daughter; now, she knew that she would be relegated to a backseat again. A lady who observed Prince Ferdinand's leave-taking from his sister commented: "The poor Duchess hardly able to let go the hand of 'my bruder'. . . . It was quite throat-lumpy."[19]

The success of his niece and nephews with Victoria prompted

Leopold himself to make a flying visit. He came full of plans for a meeting between Victoria and Albert. The beginning of October should witness their reunion, and soon after, he hoped, his plan would mature with their marriage. Victoria was dubious. She refused to commit herself to a man she had not seen for three years.

Prince Albert of Saxe-Coburg-Gotha was a handsome, well-educated, high-principled young man, only three months younger than Queen Victoria. As a child, he had been emotional and clinging, due probably to his deprivation of his mother at the age of six, and attached himself firmly to his two grandmothers, who brought him up, and to his young stepmother. His father was not averse to allowing King Leopold to supervise the education of his sons, or to the role in which Albert was cast from his youth, but he never returned the passionate devotion which Albert awarded him. There was also a close bond between the brothers, who were educated together, and were scarcely ever parted before Albert's marriage.

The Prince was most at home among his books, hated late nights and parties, despised the shallowness of 'society' and sincerely dreaded the destiny which had been allotted to him, marrying Victoria and taking his place at the head of the nation. Thus, when he arrived in England in the autumn of 1839, he was in no receptive frame of mind. He would do his duty, if Victoria so commanded him, but if she seemed the slightest bit hesitant, he would make it clear to her that he could not go on in uncertainty, and would bow out of the situation gladly, with a clear conscience.

When Victoria and Albert met, each was wary, each was rather scared. But the atmosphere soon changed. Late at night on the next day, the Queen wrote in her journal that she found Albert "fascinating". Four days later, captivated by his looks, his manners, his sharing of her love of music, his sentimentality, his deference to her, she proposed to him. Not even that honour had been left to Albert, for Victoria's rank forbade him to take the initiative. But by now, he too had come under a spell: he found Victoria all that he could have hoped. He accepted her.

For the first few days after their engagement, Victoria and

Albert kept their secret from the world. They were wrapped up in each other, and spent hours alone (aided by brother Ernest's convenient illness). Lehzen, Melbourne and Ernest were the first to be told, then Leopold and Stockmar. But Albert wrote to the latter, his former mentor: "What grieves me is that my aunt [the Duchess of Kent] to whom this important step by her daughter touches so nearly is not to know of it. But as everyone says she cannot keep her mouth shut and might even make bad use of the secret if it were entrusted to her, I quite see the necessity of it."[20] Albert wondered that anyone so fortunate as to possess a doting mother should despise the blessing. Victoria enlightened him.

It was only a few days before the Coburgs left for home that the Duchess was at last told of the engagement. She was anything but pleased. She feared the increase of King Leopold's influence through Albert, and her own further alienation from her daughter once the Prince heard of her past trials at her mother's hands. For the past few months, the Duchess of Kent had formed an alliance with the Duke and Duchess of Cambridge (who had returned from Hanover, where the Duke had been Viceroy at the time of the Duke of Cumberland's accession to the kingdom in 1837), designed to marry their son George to Victoria. Neither of the cousins had ever shown any interest in the other. George had been brought up by William IV and his Queen, and had danced with Victoria at the balls of her childhood, but there was scarcely even a friendship between them. It was bruited that the young man himself was exceedingly relieved on hearing the news that Victoria was to marry Albert.

But for all her disappointment, the Duchess of Kent might have hoped to share with Victoria the excitement of her wedding preparations. Again, however, she was pushed aside. The Queen pursued her own arrangements in her own way. Albert was far more sympathetic. He calmed the Duchess's fears that he would either ignore her or censure her for her past mistakes. An exchange of letters was soon established between them. On 21st November, Albert wrote: "Dearest Aunt, —A thousand thanks for your two dear letters, just received!

I see from them that you are in close sympathy with your nephew—your son-in-law soon to be—which gratifies me very, very much. All you say strikes me as very true, and as emanating from a heart as wise as it is kind."[21] By her efforts in remembering the Prince's attachment to motherly women, the Duchess had touched the right chord. She was to be well rewarded.

But as the wedding day (set for 10th February) approached, the long-wrangled problem of precedence began again. The Duchess begged that for that one day at least, she might have precedence over the royal English aunts. Victoria refused, and only grudgingly agreed, after consultation with Melbourne, that she might drive to the Chapel Royal with her in her carriage. The Duchess wept throughout the wedding, as she had at the Coronation. When the couple left the Chapel, it was noted by onlookers that the Queen kissed Queen Adelaide, but only shook hands with her mother.

After the wedding-breakfast, Victoria and her husband left for Windsor: "Dearest Albert came up and fetched me downstairs", she later wrote in her journal, "where we took leave of Mamma and drove off near 4; I and Albert alone."[22]

NOTES TO CHAPTER EIGHT

1 Reeve (ed.), *Greville Memoirs*, volume i, part iii, p. 403: 16.6.37.
2 Esher (ed.), *Girlhood of Queen Victoria*, volume i, p. 197: 20.6.37.
3 *Ibid.*
4 Victoria, Duchess of Kent, to Queen Victoria, 20.6.37: RA M7/68: Longford, *Victoria R.I.*, p. 83.
5 Esher (ed.), *op. cit.*, volume i, 98: 20.6.37.
6 Reeve (ed.), *op. cit.*, volume ii, part i, p. 7: 29.6.37.
7 Lord Palmerston to Princess Lieven, 28.10.37: Sudley (ed.), *Palmerston-Lieven Correspondence, 1828–58*, pp. 136–7.
8 Victoria, Duchess of Kent, to Queen Victoria, 6.11.37: RA Z482: Longford, *op. cit.*, p. 91.
9 Queen Victoria's (unpublished) journal, 2.2.39: Royal Archives: Longford, *op. cit.*, p. 121.

10 Lady Flora Hastings to the Dowager Marchioness of Hastings, 1.3.39: *Victim of Scandal*, p. 29.

11 Lord Hastings to Lord Melbourne: Creston, *Youthful Queen Victoria*, p. 368.

12 Lady Flora Hastings to Hamilton Fitzgerald, 8.3.39: *Victim of Scandal*, p. 36.

13 Lord Dunfermline to Sir John Conroy, 25.5.39: Conroy Papers, Balliol College, Oxford.

14 Duke of Wellington's memorandum, 3.6.39: *A Selection from the Private Correspondence of the Duke of Wellington*, p. 127.

15 Victoria, Duchess of Kent, to the Duke of Wellington, 3.6.39: *Ibid.*, pp. 128–9.

16 Victoria, Duchess of Kent, to Sir John Conroy, 10.6.39: Conroy Papers, Balliol College, Oxford.

17 Princess Lieven to Lady Cowper, 27.7.39: Sudley, *op. cit.*, p. 202.

18 Strachey and Fulford (ed.), *Greville Memoirs*, volume iv, p. 202.

19 Sarah Spencer, Lady Lyttelton, to Hon. Caroline Lyttelton, 12.9.39: Wyndham (ed.), *Correspondence of Sarah Spencer, Lady Lyttelton, 1787–1870*, p. 292.

20 Prince Albert to Baron Stockmar, 16.10.39: Fulford, *The Prince Consort*, pp. 43–4.

21 Prince Albert to Victoria, Duchess of Kent, 21.11.39: Jagow (ed.), *Letters of the Prince Consort*, p. 29.

22 Esher (ed.), *op. cit.*, volume ii, p. 321: 10.2.40.

CHAPTER NINE

"Grandmamma"

Was it to be "I and Albert alone" for ever? To the Duchess it might certainly seem so, despite recent indications that she would receive support from her nephew/son-in-law against her daughter's prejudice. On 15th April, she left Buckingham Palace for Ingestre House, Belgrave Square, her new home. The Duchess might well have looked forward to a dreary, lonely future—but, if she did, she was to be proved wrong. Far from closing a door, the marriage opened one to Queen Victoria's mother. With the irksome reminder of earlier days removed from her sight, the Queen could relax more in the company of her mother. With the speedy coming of a baby, she could find a new link between them. Albert helped, of course; he could see little wrong with his new 'Mamma'.

When Victoria was confined with her first child in November 1840, Albert and the Duchess together awaited the birth behind a screen in the Queen's bedroom; while Victoria recuperated, the two Coburgs dined together in a new intimacy. Thus, the third generation Victoria was a means of reconciling mother and daughter. The Duchess was invited to stand as a godmother, and three of the child's four names were her own: "Victoria Adelaide Mary Louisa."

The Duchess's transition period from perfidious *intriguante* to comforting companion, in the eyes of her daughter, was unmarked by any formal scene of reconciliation. Rather, Prince Albert worked quietly there, as in so much else, to make the Queen's life more balanced. He removed the thorns in the

(*right*) Sir John Conroy, by A. Tidey (reproduced by courtesy of the National Portrait Gallery); (*below*) "Design for a Regency", a cartoon published in 1830. Prince Leopold is dandling the future Queen Victoria on his knee while the Duchess of Kent looks on. In the adjoining room, Wellington is making a speech (reproduced by courtesy of the British Museum)

(*left*) The Duchess of Kent and Princess Victoria in 1834—a sketch by Sir George Hayter (reproduced by gracious permission of H.M. The Queen); (*right*) Victoire, Duchess of Kent in old age, by F. Winterhalter (reproduced by courtesy of the National Portrait Gallery)

path of his mother-in-law's restitution one by one. The main impediment was the Duchess's arch-enemy Lehzen, now ruling the royal nursery. However, all was not going well with the baby Princess. By the time that she was joined by a brother, the future King Edward VII, only a year after her own birth, she was found to be losing weight, despite a diet of chicken broth and ass's milk recommended by Sir James Clark. In January, she was really ill, and her parents hastened from Claremont to see her. The Prince was loudly critical of the nursery staff; the Queen, recently recovered from the birth of her son, was still suffering post-natal depression; they quarrelled. Albert turned on Lehzen, who he believed had neglected his child.

This was not an isolated incident. Ever since the marriage, Albert had resented the former governess's position about his wife. Victoria's gratitude to Lehzen for her help in the pre-accession years at Kensington had not waned; she had been the Princess's only ally when she was bitterly at a loss for help. Her continuance with the Queen as her confidante had been her reward, and before the marriage she had never abused the position. She was popular with members of the Court, and grateful to any who befriended her; she had never tried to influence the Queen politically, but had dove-tailed neatly with Melbourne in dominating Victoria's life. But with the advent of Albert, the problem of Lehzen's position had begun to trouble everyone, not least the Prince himself. He was insecure in his new role, not allowed to help the Queen in her statecraft (he merely blotted her signature to documents), only beginning to find himself a niche in the organization of the Queen's private business and in the administration of Buckingham Palace. While he deferred to Melbourne's superior judgment on British politics, he could not help but envy Lehzen her assurance in the Queen's dependence on her. And for herself, Lehzen was jealous of the new element in the Queen's emotional life.

Thus, when Albert came to believe that Lehzen was actually putting his child's life in jeopardy, he threw caution to the winds. He let Victoria know how much he mistrusted Lehzen, and wrote to Stockmar, "Lehzen is a crazy, common, stupid intriguer, obsessed with lust of power, who regards herself as a demi-god, and anyone who refuses to acknowledge her as such, as a criminal."[1] Albert's outburst drew from Victoria a similar display of passion: quarrels raged until peacemaker Stockmar intervened. He presented to the Queen, in so cool a manner that she must see reason, the dilemma which faced the Prince in finding himself a place in England, and in combating Lehzen for her trust. Immediately, she was all apologies and excuses, and admitted that there was room for improvement in the nursery regime.

Six months later, Albert informed his wife that Lehzen intended to visit her old home in Germany, "for her health". The parting was made easy: Lehzen stayed with the children while Victoria and Albert went to Scotland. By the time they returned, she was gone.

There can be no doubt but that the Duchess of Kent was glad to see the departure of the woman she had brought to England more than twenty years previously, and who had played such a major part in separating her from her daughter. It was difficult not to blame Lehzen for Victoria's thwarting of Conroy's plans: had Lehzen not guided and strengthened the child, the Duchess and Sir John might have triumphed in forcing her to sign away her rights to them. Well might the Duchess of Kent enjoy Lehzen's present disgrace. But it was a hard fate for Victoria's friend, who in fact never returned to England, and who lived on until 1870 to see her former charge, though always affectionate and allowing her to want for no material good, completely freed from her influence.

By the time that Lehzen left, Melbourne had been long gone —gone from office, that is, and almost completely dropped from the Queen's home life. As early as May 1841, Prince Albert had privately come to terms with Peel so that there should be no renewal of the Bedchamber controversy when he came into power. When the new Government was installed that September, there was no storm from the Queen. Melbourne, however, did not take his dismissal so lightly. For three years he had lived only for this daughter-substitute; now he could not bear to be parted from her. For a time, frequent visits kept them together, then a correspondence; then, gradually, the Queen's growing respect for and trust in Peel, and the increased influence of Albert, saw the end of the exchange of letters with her old mentor. Melbourne died in 1848. It was not for many years, until the publication of the *Greville Memoirs* in the 1870s and '80s that the Queen realized how much of her supposedly confidential talks with her Prime Minister the latter had retailed at the dinner tables of London society. By then, her girlish infatuation forgotten, she was ready to censure her former idol.

With both Lehzen and Melbourne swept away, Victoria's life became more and more centred on her family—with Albert at the head of the household, and with her mother permitted an increasingly central role as grandmother to the royal brood.

After the baptism of the Princess Royal in January 1841, the next great event in the Duchess of Kent's life was her five months' trip to the Continent, which began that May. It was the first time that she had been abroad since her husband had brought her to England in 1819, and she made the most of it. First came a visit to her brother Leopold, in his regal state in Belgium, then a journey into her brother's Ernest's duchies, with fêtes and entertainments in her honour. An English magazine, *The World of Fashion*, regaled its lady readers with details of a more poignant home-coming: "The Duchess arrived on the 5th of July at Amorbach, the seat of the Prince of Leiningen, at which her Royal Highness's youthful days were passed, and whence the Duchess had been absent twenty-two years. The whole population of the place and neighbourhood went out to meet her, and escorted her home with every token of the most affectionate welcome. The Duchess shed tears at this kind demonstration."[2]

Amorbach had not changed—except in its prosperity; the once-familiar palace was looking brighter—by dint of the Duchess's own generosity to her son and by the gift of a new block on the market-square by the townspeople at the time of his marriage. One can well imagine how the Duchess felt, after so long an absence, on returning to her old home. She wrote to Queen Victoria: "It is like a dream that I am writing to you from this place. My heart is so full. I am occupied with you and Albert and the precious little creature. I was quite upset by the kind reception the poor people here gave me. Everywhere I found proofs of affection and gratitude. I occupy the rooms where your dear father lived."[3]

Other holidays abroad were to follow in the next few years; in the spring of 1844, the Duchess went to Paris, *incognita* as the Countess of Dublin, and then on to Switzerland to stay with her sister Juliana, who was still living out the lonely existence she had chosen so many years before. In June of the following year, the Duchess of Kent was at Coburg to receive Victoria and Albert, on the former's first visit to Germany. This was a link indeed between the two Victorias—the 'togetherness' of the Coburgs, in which the Queen's place was earned as much by virtue of her mother as through her husband. Both the Duchess and the Prince could claim the hometown as their birthplace.

And now it was possible to devote time and attention to her Leiningen children, whereas before, the Duchess had been too preoccupied with her English daughter to give them more than loving letters, sincere blessings, good advice—and money.

Prince Charles of Leiningen had always been a problem. Without a father from the age of nine, without his mother's presence since he was fourteen, he had become a wild, self-willed young man—who had been only too eager to enter the intrigues of Kensington Palace for his own future advancement. Married to a woman with whom his only tie now was a long-since-spent passion, he was consoling himself with a series of amorous misadventures. Since 1829, he had been accepting from his mother all the money that she could afford to send him, restoring not only his home at Amorbach but the family hunting lodge, some eight miles away in the pine woods, Waldleiningen. Thus, when Sir George Couper managed to wrest Conroy's account books from the Duchess in 1850, he found not only blank pages for many years' worth of entries, but that £60,000 of the Duchess's income could not be accounted for as to its expending. It is not only to the peculations of Sir John Conroy that one must look, though they were extensive enough, but to the Duchess's generosity to her son.

She would have done better to have made a generous allowance to her daughter Feodora, whose princely state at Langenburg would have been regarded as penury by even the minor English aristocracy. As King Leopold wrote to Queen Victoria in 1840: "She really is too poor; when one thinks that they have but £600 a year, and that large castles, etc. are to be kept up with it, one cannot conceive how they manage it."[4] Feodora had had six children between 1829 and 1839: Charles, Hermann, Victor, Eliza, Adelaide and Feodora, all of whom must have proper provision made for them if they were to live in the manner of princes and make suitable marriages.

The Hohenlohes managed to give the boys an education at the universities of Dresden and Berlin, but then there was the question of careers for Hermann and Victor who must make their own fortunes. Hermann took service in the Austrian army, through the interest of his Mensdorff relations, while Queen Victoria offered Victor a cadetship in the British Navy. (He was soon joined by his cousin Ernest of Leiningen—it was a good moment for the boy to leave home, for his father had recently separated from his wife, and was devoting himself to a life of indolent debauchery.) During the war with Russia of the mid-1850s, Victor Hohenlohe saw active service in the Baltic and the Crimea: in 1854, the Queen sent telegrams to her sister reassuring her of her son's safety, when he took part in the bombardment of Bomarsund in the Alund Islands, designed to destroy Russia's Baltic fleet; and in the following summer, when he was with a naval assault group besieging Sebastopol, Victor contracted and—rare luck—survived cholera in the Crimea. He remained in British service for the rest of his life, with the family title 'Count Gleichen', married his Admiral's daughter, Laura Seymour, and raised a large family of children who were playmates of the young royal family.

Charles Hohenlohe was a real Coburg-Leiningen in his propensity for mischief and *amours* (the Hohenlohe forebears were reputedly very solid citizens), and troubled his staid father until

Prince Ernest's death in 1860. Thereafter he renounced his in-heritance, and married a village girl, Marie Grathwohl, with whom he had been associating for years. Prince Hermann, with his background of military discipline, made a much more suit-able ruler of the family's estates.

The Hohenlohe daughters, though in themselves docile and obedient, were rather more of a problem than their brothers. Their dowries would be small enough, but their relationship to the British throne was attractive bait to potential suitors. The girls were often in England, at Windsor with their aunt Vic-toria or staying with their grandmother at Frogmore (the house on the Windsor estate which the Duchess of Kent received from the Crown on the death of the Princess Augusta in Sep-tember 1839). And with Queen Victoria's fears that her own daughters had no suitable playmates, the Hohenlohe girls filled the gap to her satisfaction. In 1851, the eldest daughter, Eliza, died, to the great grief of her grandmother, with whom she had been a favourite. The following year, the family came sadly to England, but when the parents returned home, Ada (the Princess Adelaide) remained behind in the Duchess's care. Ernest and Feodora travelled *via* Paris, staying a few days there amid the excitement of the birth of the Second Empire, before continuing the long road home. On 2nd December, the Prince-President, Louis-Napoleon Bonaparte, was proclaimed Napoleon III, Emperor of the French, and his ambassador, Count Walew-ski, offered his new credentials to the English Queen. Within a week, letters were flying between England and Langenburg: the Emperor had proposed, through Walewski, for the hand of the Princess Adelaide of Hohenlohe-Langenburg. Nothing was said to the girl while the great debate between her elders went on. It was obvious that the Emperor wished to be allied with the English royal House, but as the Queen's eldest daughter was only a child and could not in any case, become a Catholic on her marriage (which was a necessary preliminary to the match) without forfeiting her rights to inherit, the next best was the Queen's niece.

Victoria was adamant against an alliance with the *parvenus* Bonapartes; and was she not herself sheltering the Orleanist

King of France and his family at Claremont? Feodora was
equally set against the match. But, with the enlightenment of
the age, young Ada must be given her chance if she had any
desire to become an empress. Feodora wrote to her mother and
to the Queen, begging them to inform her daughter of the proposal, to make her aware of the drawbacks as well as the
delights of the great position and to do their best to dissuade
her if she was inclined to accept. Ada was dutiful; the Emperor's
honour was politely declined. Some time later, she was to marry
Frederick of Schleswig-Holstein-Augustenburg, one of the contenders in the war for the possession of the duchies of
Schleswig-Holstein in the 1860s, and was to become the mother
of Augusta Victoria who married Kaiser Wilhelm II of Germany. Her younger sister Feodora married the widower George,
Duke of Saxe-Meiningen, a cousin on her father's side of the
family. Through all the Hohenlohe marriages, the name Feodora
is seen to crop up in the children again and again, so that what
was, before the matriarch Feodora's birth, an unknown form
of the old Russian patronimic, became a rather common name
among the many 'serene highnesses' of old Germany.

Apart from her few Continental trips, the Duchess of Kent
lived mainly at Frogmore between 1840 and 1850. She had
the company of the younger generation, but her contemporaries among the royal family were dying off. The Duke of
Cumberland lived as ruler of Hanover until 1851; the Duke
of Cambridge enjoyed an eccentric old age until 1850; Princess
Mary survived them all, dying as late as 1857—but all the
other royal dukes and princesses had long since gone to their
graves. In 1849, good Queen Adelaide died. In the last few
years, the Duchess of Kent's self-created feud with her sister-
in-law had been obliterated; the early days of their English
marriages were renewed. Wholly without rancour, and united
with the Duchess in love of the Queen, Adelaide accepted without question her old friend's return, and it would be in
character if she never mentioned the rifts of her husband's reign.
Only a month before Queen Adelaide's death, the Duchess had
been staying with her at Bushey.

In 1854, another old friend died: Sir John Conroy. At last, the Queen and the Duchess could discuss him with equanimity. The Duchess admitted that he had done great harm; the Queen conceded, "I will not speak of the *past* and of the many sufferings he entailed on me by creating divisions between you and me wh. wd. never have existed otherwise; they are buried with him. For his poor wife and Children I am truly sorry. They are now free from the *ban* wh. kept them from ever appearing before me."[5] The Duchess now proved her loyalty to Conroy and assisted his impecunious family; she continued her affectionate interest in them in a copious correspondence. At her mother's death, the Queen continued to pay their allowances. But Victoria never renewed acquaintance with her former companion, Victoire.

By that time, the Queen and the Duchess could view the past without the revival of old emotions. The mother of a sometimes-difficult family, the Queen could more readily understand how much her own mother had had to bear from her in the 1830s. Now that the Duchess of Kent (seventy in 1856) had mellowed, she was regarded as a lovable, if rather simple-minded old lady. Until about that time, she had kept up her musical performances, and one of her own compositions had been played to celebrate the Prince of Wales's birth. Now, with increased frailty, her hobbies were more passive—collecting trinkets and 'novelties', coloured prints and 'ornaments'. The lap-dogs and bright-plumed birds in which she had rejoiced in her youth still figured largely in her old-age endearments. And, as a courtier was to reminisce later, she still played cards: "We used to stay at Frogmore with the Duchess of Kent. She liked whist; she would play a card, and take a transitory nap, and we were quite happy to wait till she woke and picked up the trick, which she did with dignity and very deftly. She was very kind. She used to pity me me for having to inhale the 'Fogues' [fogs] of London."[6] Another witness to the Duchess's game-playing—and to her inability, after more than thirty years in England, to master the language—is Lady Lyttelton, governess to the royal children: "Last night we played Blind Hookey, a horrid gambling game, for pence. And the Duchess of Kent quite innocently asked: 'Blind Hookey? What is dat name?' 'I don't know,' said the Prince [Albert], 'only he is Hookey, and he is blind.' So we laughed, it was said so gravely, and quite puzzled the Duchess.'"[7]

Life was good for a well-to-do old lady in the nineteenth century; a royal duchess enjoyed all the benefits of her contemporaries—deference, comfort, unceasing attention—and, besides, had all the little excitements of the Court to amuse her. When foreign royalties visited, she shared the entertainments; on a State occasion, she donned ermine and coronet and acknowledged the cheers of the populace; she met the great and the famous, and appreciated them according to her own lights. If the detailed events of the Duchess's life in the years 1840–55 seem sparse, it is because they were happy years, though it is also due to the fact that she was then without a close biographer in her household. From the early 1850s, however, a devoted lady-in-waiting and a lively writer, Lady Augusta Bruce, was sending home letters which shed light on the last years of Queen Victoria's mother.

In 1850, in her early sixties, the Duchess discovered a new interest with a new home, Abergeldie Castle, near Balmoral, in Scotland. She was to stay there for part of the year over the next eight years. A local woman, Patricia Lindsay, recalled many years later "the image of a stout, comely, elderly lady, whose face overflowed with kindliness and good humour, quietly dignified, yet with a gentle courtesy that set even a shy child at ease". There was a "sprightly old German Baroness de Spaet [sic], full of lively sallies in her quaint broken English, often pretending to misunderstand in order to raise a laugh at her own expense", and another lady-in-waiting "devoted to dogs, and firmly believing in their possession of souls and prospect of a future life—an opinion much strengthened, she told me, by having once seen the ghost of Lambkin, the Duchess's white poodle, after that royal favourite had departed for the happy hunting-grounds of his race".

Patricia Lindsay notes that music and card-playing were the order of the day, after dinner. And the Duchess could still show herself a fine performer on the piano. More lively entertainment came on royal birthdays, when there was generally a dance given for tenants and servants. The Duchess, dressed in white and wearing a lace cap with ribbons, watched the merriment from a dais, as ladies and visiting gentry performed reels and jigs with footmen and ghillies. "The Duchess sat smiling kindly upon the pleasure of her guests of all degrees, and evidently enjoying the merriment, which her presence kept within due bounds."[8]

Here is Lady Augusta Bruce's account of another birthday, celebrated at Abergeldie in 1853:

. . . . roused by the National Anthem in full chorus I rushed to the window of my little room and there beheld at the door of the tower, under H.R.H.'s bedroom windows, the whole household congregated—Maslin in the front in full rig, bouquet in buttonhole, music in hand, leading the band—very Costa! and there stood my Tuppin, my Tustin, my Seabrook, with his wideawake befeathered, and even our Hallan, our Ogg, awed by the gravity of the circumstances into something unlike his usual waggishness! It was very pretty, all the maids with bouquets, and all so neat and tidy. At the conclusion of the anthem, Captain Gordon's keeper, a great talent and a very handsome fellow, struck up some appropriate tunes and marched up and down with great dignity. We assembled in the dining room to greet the Duchess, who appeared in white looking very well, and accompanied by the family. By this time I was longing for my coffee, but there is many a slip between the cup and the lip, and this I was destined to experience, for in came Seabrook and recited an ode of his own in honour of H.R.H.—really extremely pretty —of course I was too shy to look at anything but my empty plate, and felt very hot, especially when at the conclusion, after many 'Thees and Thines' came suddenly 'Y.R. 'ighness'. It was too dear, and I assure you the thing was neat and clear to a degree, but that pronunciation at such a moment rather perilled the composure of my overwrought nerves. Then came the anthem again, a cheer, and breakfast, but in the middle the pipes struck up once more, and the gillies appeared in profusion, followed by the labourers, all carrying flags and wreaths and whatnot— another pause, the end of breakfast, and then on the lawn and in the dining room a reel or two, danced by the new 'Duncan' doing wonders at the sword dances. After this we came upstairs, the men having first given a Gaelic toast in honour of H.R.H.—

The drawing-room table was decorated as usual with lovely wreaths, and covered with presents. . . . I must say I thought my vase looked as pretty and more chaste than anything . . . but the nicest present was that of Princess Feo., a charming child of 13, chosen by herself at the Hague, in the neighbourhood of which place she has been staying for the bathing, and from whence she only arrived yesterday, travelled all alone in her grandeur with her attendants. This present she wrote asking her Mama's leave to buy, praising its *lovliness*. It is a sort of pen tray supported by two most funny looking bears on their hind legs. . . .[9]

A highlight of the 1856 holiday was the visit of Florence Nightingale, a national heroine since her nursing exertions during the Crimean War. Lady Augusta was glad

to see the dear Duchess' delight.—"It seems to me like a dream to see her there," and many such outbursts.—After dinner H.R.H. confided to me that she had wished to propose her health, but was too shy!!! . . . Poor Miss N. would have been tolerably overpowered—it was just as well.—The Duchess abandoned the card-table that night and sat talking to her all the evening without sleepiness.[10]

But since the middle years of the 1850s, all the Duchess's pleasure was tempered by the almost constant pain in her body. She had been ill for some time before it was diagnosed as cancer. And from the summer of 1856, there was the additional torment of muscular rheumatism, which vied with the other pain, and was but a prelude to more widespread stiffness. Again and again, in her letters to her sister, Lady Augusta writes of the devotion which the Duchess's patience in her sufferings draws from her. Even when contemplating marriage, she puts aside the idea—completely voluntarily—to remain with her:

The Duchess said: "I wish you all happiness some day, but you must not leave me, you must stay with me while I live" . . . my feelings, how I was nearly choked and could say nothing—I did not understand at first, for I was so far from thinking of any personal use of the advice—Oh! the beloved—I felt that even if I had wish to leave, I could not have harboured it for a moment after that—it touched me so deeply, and made me so unutterably thankful, for you know that I have not a desire beyond my two present duties, and think it is so difficult for me to fancy that I can do these aright, and each grave look I see,

I fancy, as you know, that all is wrong, therefore the encouragement is doubly precious, and to be able to pour out my sense of it to you is a relief. I kissed the dear hand. . . .[11]

Inevitably, for the Duchess became a septuagenarian in 1856, family deaths troubled otherwise happy years. But one death, that of her son in 1856, was totally unexpected until a short time before. With his wife far away and uncaring, Charles of Leiningen died on 13th November 1856, with only his sister Feodora to comfort him. Breaking the news to the family in England, Feodora wrote to Victoria:

Our dear brother is no more. I have closed his eyes: he is at rest. . . . We have lost a dear brother: he loved you and me with all his heart. Dearest, dearest Victoria, I kiss your hands with many tears. . . . Alas, dearest sister, I can hardly think it possible that it was he I saw dying, that he is lying dead in this house. . . . He had been so well and cheerful at Langenburg only three months ago. I am so glad I saw so much of him during the last years of his life.[12]

Lady Augusta Bruce, 19th November:

The Duchess is wonderfully strengthened and upheld in body and mind—Her precious health is better in all essentials than it has been lately, though, as might be expected, H.R.H. suffers much from nervous headache and pain over the left eye.—The excitement, the speaking, seeing the family, and worst of all, those terrible letters, keep up a constant agitation that prevents the nerves recovering their tone. Rest, rest, rest is what her worn heart and spirit require and call for—and gradually it will come. The very sorrow seems like a frightful dream, so little has she been able to look at it alone and quietly, and to realize it. . . . On Sunday evg. the beloved Queen came all alone to her.—Can you fancy Her coming out of a carriage and going into it again *quite alone*? The Princess and I both felt that we could not trust Her and must jump in as one would do with a Baby.—Her kindness, Her anxiety, the tenderness, are too dear, but we are rather in the dark I imagine as to how to set about dealing with people, in the Duchess's state! Oh! the beloved [the Queen]—Thank God she has not had much experience.—To have seen her trotting up to the Baroness' room . . . then trotting about Her Mama and bringing pictures of the Prince and of his horses, and every possible detail and account—and so sad Herself, weeping so bitterly, but not before Mama to upset her.[13]

All the Queen's former resentment against her brother for his 'treachery' of 1837 had long since melted away: her disapproval of his morality and his way of life turned to pity. Prince Albert, however, always more prudish than his wife, could not pass up this opportunity of drawing a moral from the misfortunes of others. Charles's alienation from his wife drew from him the last word on the subject: "Marie Leiningen is in Rome and she lives in a poor lodging. Mr Spare, her cavalier, married her lady's maid. A sad result of the theory of life which Charles always preached, that life was for enjoyment and that the wisest thing was not to consider anyone else."[14]

Family visits, births and marriages are a powerful balm to grief, and the Duchess of Kent was to enjoy several such easements in the next few years. Shortly afterwards, in January 1858, Victoria, the Princess Royal, married Frederick William of Prussia, son of the Crown Prince, and it is with an exchange of letters between Queen Victoria and her eldest daughter in Germany that this chapter must close. In December 1858, the Queen wrote to her "dearest child":

By the by, Grandmamma is *en peine* about a commission, she gave to Fritz some time ago, about a screen which he was to have made up for you for Xmas. Grandmamma sent the work for it (two Highlanders) in October with a letter to Fritz and he has never answered it, or acknowledged the screen or anything. Now Fritz is so punctual, never forgetting anything, that I don't understand it—and wish you to be sure and ask him about it as it distresses Grandmamma.[15]

A prompt reply from Berlin brought only annoyance: "Your Grandmamma is in despair at Fritz's mistake in making up the screen as a cushion and he must write and defend himself. Grandmamma says he never gave her any answer."[16]

NOTES TO CHAPTER NINE

1   Prince Albert to Baron Stockmar, 16.1.42: RA Vic Add MSS U2: Longford, *Victoria R.I.*, p. 200.
2   *World of Fashion*, July 1841, p. 187–8.

3 Gurney, *Childhood of Queen Victoria*, pp. 32–3.
4 Leopold, King of the Belgians, to Queen Victoria, 22.5.40: Albert, *Queen Victoria's Sister*, p. 103.
5 Queen Victoria to Victoria, Duchess of Kent, 2.3.54: Longford, *op. cit.*, p. 146.
6 Locker-Lampson, *My Confidences*, p. 154.
7 Sarah Spencer, Lady Lyttelton, to Hon. Caroline Lyttelton, 16.8.46: Wyndham (ed.), *Letters of Sarah Spencer, Lady Lyttelton, 1787–1870*, pp. 360–1.
8 Quotations from Lindsay, *Recollections of a Royal Parish*, pp. 82–6.
9 Lady Augusta Bruce to Lady Frances Baillie, 17.8.53: Bolitho and Baillie (ed.), *Letters of Lady Augusta Stanley, 1849–63*, pp. 53–5.
10 *Ibid.*, 5.10.56: *Ibid.*, p. 106.
11 *Ibid.*, 20.8.57: *Ibid.*, p. 118.
12 Feodora, Princess of Hohenlohe-Langenburg, to Queen Victoria, 13.11.56: Albert, *op. cit.*, p. 156.
13 Lady Augusta Bruce to Lady Frances Baillie, 19.11.56: Bolitho and Baillie (ed.), *op. cit.*, pp. 114–5.
14 Prince Albert to Ernest, Duke of Saxe-Coburg-Gotha, November 1856: Albert, *op. cit.*, p. 156.
15 Queen Victoria to Princess Victoria of Prussia, 29.12.58: Fulford (ed.), *Dearest Child*, pp. 153–4.
16 *Ibid.*, 5.1.59: *Ibid.*, p. 156.

CHAPTER TEN

Epitaph for a Duchess

In May 1859 the Duchess of Kent's ill-health came to a crisis. Shortly before leaving Frogmore to go to Windsor for the Queen's birthday, she felt feverish—later symptoms were diagnosed as those of erysipelas. The Queen was instantly alerted; for a time it was feared that the Duchess would die. But, violent as the early stages of the illness seem, they are comparatively quick to pass. By the 25th, Queen Victoria was able to write to her uncle Leopold:

Thank God! to-day I feel another being for we know she is "in a satisfactory state", and improving in every respect, but I am thoroughly shaken and upset by this *awful* shock; for it came on so *suddenly*—that it came like a thunder-bolt upon us, and I think I *never* suffered as I did those four dreadful hours till we heard she was better! I hardly myself *knew how* I loved her, or how *my whole* existence seems bound up with her—till I saw looming in the distance the fearful possibility of *what* I will *not* mention. She was actually packing up to start for here! *How* I missed her yesterday I cannot say, or how gloomy my poor birthday on first getting up appeared I *cannot* say. However, that is passed—and please God we shall see her, with care, restored to her usual health ere long.[1]

Though the Duchess was convalescing cheerfully by mid-June, her doctors were still worried as to the effect her recent illness might have had on her already low constitution. By the end of the month, she was forced to agree to give up her annual holiday at Abergeldie, and settle for a short stay at Cramond, near Edinburgh, in what the Queen was to call a "really charming residence . . . quite near the sea, with beautiful trees, and very cheerful".[2]

Eighteen hundred and sixty proved to be a year of sharp contrast: a host of family visits were saddened by the death of Ernest of Hohenlohe-Langenburg, Feodora's husband, in April, and that of the Grand Duchess Juliana in August. Only the Duchess of Kent and her brother Leopold remained of the happy family of Coburg. Now, her life was to be bound more closely with the happiness of her remaining children and her grandchildren. And in 1861, on the anniversary of his marriage, Prince Albert paid tribute to the Duchess's devotion:

I cannot let this day go by without writing to you, even if I had not to thank you for your kind wishes and the charming photographs. Twenty-one years make a good long while, and to-day our marriage "comes of age, according to law". We have faithfully kept our pledge for better and for worse, and have only to thank God, that He has vouchsafed so much happiness to us. May He have us in His keeping for the days to come! You have, I trust, found good and loving children in us, and we have experienced nothing but love and kindness from you.

In the hope that your pains and aches will now leave you soon, I remain, as ever, Your affectionate son, Albert.[3]

At the beginning of the last week in February, the Duchess was able to go out, and was talking of leaving Frogmore for London, but on the 25th she had a bad night and the next day, Tuesday 26th, "she took an attack of indigestion, and the right arm, which has long been swollen, began to inflame in a most alarming way".[4] On 6th March, the surgeon came, and on the 9th lanced the abscess, which gave some relief. A few days later, the Queen visited her mother, and though she "did not shew She was struck by Her looking ill . . . she was very sad on going home".[5]

For a time, the Duchess seemed to be getting stronger, though it still wrung Lady Augusta's heart to see her suffering: "The dear left hand and face and body were so thin—the pain in the back had decreased, and in the breast was scarcely at all."[6] Then, on the 15th, the doctors recognized the symptoms of imminent death. The Queen was informed immediately of her mother's condition:

They arrived at 7, alas! too late to be recognized, but had they been sooner, I am sure that nothing would have been said, the Duchess was too weak to enjoy—would have grieved that they should see Her so ill, and wished that they should only return when She was better. It was a sad, sad trial to the Queen, but to Her a mercy. She was indeed ready, and She was gently removed to where the pang of parting would be unfelt—and saved all the physical suffering. Ladies Ely, Grey, Biddulph,—others I do not remember came—dinner was served at 9.30 in dining room, and for the Queen later in the flower room. I sat in the colonnade alone till dinner, and was most thankful to be called away during it, to go and see about rooms and beds and for the 2 Princesses and Pss. Alice—the latter was on my sofa in my middle room —Patterson, her maid, on my bed—the Queen in the scarlet fever room with the maid Weiss—the Prince in the room at the other end, North, also.—That settled, I returned to the bedroom, where Lady Fanny came. The Beloved had then Her nightcap on, and all arranged, but we had great difficulty in getting off the crinoline etc. etc., and even with cushions it was very difficult to get Her comfortably placed on the sofa, owing to the arm and different wounds. The eyes still opened and looked anxiously around—the hand pointed mechanically to little things wanted, and from time to time seemed to indicate the discomfort of the position.—No one was very clever about remedying this—Clark and Brown feared to alter it, and it was not till evg. that by dint of pressing they were persuaded with a shawl to lift Her into a more comfortable position.—

The dear Prince was most efficient. After that there was not a symptom of malaise, and I rejoiced to think that the arm She loved so much was the one to obtain this. He was so tender. The poor Queen had promised to try and rest till She was called, but She could not—three times She stole down with Her little lamp and Weiss, in Her white dressing gown, and knelt kissing the hand and whispering "Mama" so lovingly and earnestly as if the sound must rouse Her.—

At one moment Elise and I thought there was some consciousness—she told Her it was me, but alas! there was no real response, only a half answer in the eye.—She took spoonsful of wine and water the poor Queen some sal volatile. I did not feel in the least tired—I lay on the floor at times—Lady F. sat in an armchair—Anne, Elise and Marie were about in turn. At 4.30 some tea was given us, which made me feel worse—at 6, or before, the Queen returned dressed, and the Prince. The cold grey dawn aroused the birds—soon we began to see the gardeners appear, and the workmen who are engaged on the sad Mausoleum.—It was very chilly, as a window in the adjoining room was open.—The Dr. dressed the poor wounds—a long business. Lady F. and I went into the sitting room where all was left as the day before—you could not believe She was not coming in, and you were waiting for Her.—The Queen was in the North sitting room upstairs. The dressing over, we all returned—I continued to give the wine and water—the others stood or sat round. All was still—only the ticking and striking of the clock watch the Queen used to hear in Her childhood. Almost all the things in the bedroom were Kensington things, or older, and the Queen had scarcely seen them since.—The pulse grew feebler and feebler—Brown or Clark came in from time to time and felt it—towards 9, as I gave a spoonful, something which I believe is the death rattle seemed to threaten to choke the beloved invalid, though She still opened Her mouth and swallowed.— I did not venture to give any more, and we all knelt and watched —the breathing was soft and low—the intervals between each breath were longer—very long—and at last *all was over*.[7]

The Queen's emotions were shattered by her mother's death. Amid paroxysms of grief, she wrote to her uncle Leopold:

My dearly beloved Uncle,—On this, the most dreadful day of my life, does your poor broken-hearted child write one line of love and devotion. *She* is gone. That *precious, dearly beloved tender* Mother—whom I never was parted from but for a few months—without whom *I* can't *imagine life*—has been taken from us! It is *too* dreadful! But she is at peace—at rest—her fearful sufferings at an end! It was quite painless—though there was very *distressing*, heartrending breathing to witness. I held her dear, dear hand in mine to the very last, which I am truly thankful for! But the watching that precious life going out was fearful! Alas! she never knew me! But she was spared the pang of parting! How this will *grieve* and *distress you*. *You* who are now doubly precious to us. Good Alice was with us all through, and deeply afflicted, and wishes to say everything kind to you. Bertie and Lenchen are now here—all much grieved, and have seen her *sleeping* peacefully and eternally! Dearest Albert is dreadfully overcome and well he may, for she adored him! I feel so truly *verwaist*. God bless and protect you. Ever your devoted and truly unhappy Niece and Child.

Victoria R[8]

In the days that followed, the Queen returned again and again to her mother's house, giving the excuse that work on the mausoleum, still incomplete at her death, must be hurried along. The Frogmore mausoleum was a compromise: the Duchess "had wanted to rest at Coburg but consented to stay here if she cd: have a little tenement of her own—everyone knows that the first object of planners of cemeteries & builders of vaults is a dry soil, but these good folks have selected a marsh and it appears that a fire must be kept in the mausoleum thro'out all seasons to keep off decay. I heard that the P[rince] of W[ales] said he wd: take good care not to be buried in such a place."[9]

For a few days, the Duchess's body remained at Frogmore, lying in state in the drawing-room. The room was hung with black drapes, and furnished with black chairs, but everywhere there were flowers, white and purple, and palm branches and wreaths. The coffin was covered with a black pall with armorial bearings embroidered in large squares, and on top rested the Duchess of Kent's coronet on a cushion. At 4 am the following Monday, the body was removed to St George's Chapel, Windsor, and at 11 am the interment took place there—a temporary measure until the mausoleum should be finished. The Queen wrote to her uncle: "I and our daughters did not go *yesterday* [to the funeral]—it would have been *far* too much for *me*—and Albert when he returned, with tearful eyes told me it was well I did not go—so affecting had been the sight—*so* universal the sympathy."[10]

A welcome distraction for the Queen, but a trying task to the Prince Consort, was the sorting and dividing among the family of the Duchess's personal belongings. Although the Duchess had left most of her tangible property to the Queen, there were several bequests to servants and friends from her collection of trinkets and *bibelots*, all nested individually in silver foil. Victoria wrote sadly to her eldest daughter:

Every evening we are occupied with the dear papers. The preliminary sorting is finished—and now remains the arranging of those that are sorted. Such touching relics I have found! Her love for me is beyond everything! Not a scrap of my writing—

or of my hair has ever been thrown away—and such touching notes in a book about my babyhood. We found a most precious relic of my poor father, which I had never seen. His little writing desk—with his Garter purse, the drawing of the room he died in—his three last letters to dearest Mama (in French) and such loving, tender letters, and a little book of hers in which she wrote in every week after his death expressive of such love and tender affection for him—such despair at his death, such longing to be soon re-united to him! It is so touching to see! And now after forty-one years they are re-united, and both surely bless their poor orphan child! Yes, and she trusts one day to be everlastingly with them. That is a blessed thought and one which I love to dwell on—much as I love to remain in this world for the many very precious ones I possess![11]

It came as a surprise to many that "The Duchess is *said* to have left only £25,000 which is divided between the Hohenlohes and Leiningens. Considering that for twenty-two years the Duchess has been in receipt of £30,000 per annum, and that her mode of living was extremely retired, it is difficult to believe that she has not died more rich."[12] The comparatively small sum which the Duchess left is, of course, accounted for by the continuous draining of her income to her late son in Germany, and in numerous smaller gifts to her grandchildren, but also to some extent by her benevolence to several charities. One such was the 'Augusta Endowment', King Leopold's foundation of 1832, in memory of his mother, for "first, the educating [of] a number of indigent girls; on the 19th of January every year (that day having been the birthday of this excellent Princess) providing a poor maiden, of irreproachable conduct, with a sum of fifty florins as an outfit; the furnishing maintenance to a meritorious and competent female in the capacity of teacher; and lastly, the providing a boy of good character and talent, with indentures of apprenticeship and the requisite outfit".[13] In the same year, the Duchess had set up a school for fifty of the children of Esher, near her brother's house of Claremont.

Many years later, Queen Victoria was to entrust her mother's diaries to Lady Augusta Bruce, who noted: "These contain, as Your Majesty knows, dry daily facts, and the few purely personal remarks which enable one to trace, by inference, the touching outward and inward struggle, thro' which that devoted, sensitive, maternal heart regained the peace and joy and confidence that had been destroyed by the timidity which allowed a third person to come between mother and child."[14] That letter was written in 1874, but even by the time of the Duchess's death, the Queen had driven from her mind all thought of blame that her mother had made so much of her childhood unhappy. She remembered only the last years and the close bond which she and her mother had belatedly shared:

> Oh! I am so wretched to think *how, for a time, two people most* wickedly estranged us! . . . To miss a mother's friendship —not to be able to have her to confide in—when a girl *most* needs it, was fearful! I *dare* not think of it—it drives me *wild* now! But thank God! that is all passed *long, long ago*, and she had forgotten it, and only thought of the last very happy years.
> And all that was brought by my good angel, dearest Albert, whom *she* adored, and in whom she had such unbounded confidence. . . .[15]

With the return to London, soon after the funeral, came duties which the Queen found extremely distasteful and tended to resent. One such was the renewal of her attendance at 'drawing-rooms'; the first of these was to be a 'black drawing-room', at which the debutantes wore the traditional white, but mothers and chaperones were obliged to wear mourning as a condition of their admittance. One of the elder ladies present was Miss Agnes Strickland, a popular writer of the time, who described the scene at the 'black drawing-room' to her mother:

> You will be glad to hear that I got through the black drawing-room yesterday quite well. I wore a black velvet train, black silk underdress, and a black velvet tiara, lappets and plume. I fear that head-dress must have given me the look of Bellona. However, as everybody wore the same style of headgear, it did not much signify; but I found it very hot and heavy. The young ladies who were presented were all costumed in lily-white with garlands and bouquets of flowers of the same spotless hue. It was really a fine sight to see these grand black dresses and sable plumes, blazing with diamonds, intermingled with the white dresses of the young ladies.
> The Queen looked out of health. It must have been a great

trial to her to be in a manner compelled to appear in public after her great sorrow. There was an immense crowd; and but for the assistance of Lord Talbot de Malahide, who got the carriage up for me, I should never have got through the crush.[16]

That summer was very trying for the Queen, and many people, like Miss Strickland, reported her out of health. Her excesses of grief at her mother's death—and the even more intense mourning after that of her husband—have been criticized by some biographers as signs of neurosis and weakness of character; others have stressed more charitably the contemporary customs of mourning and the prevalence of long-term bereavement of all classes in the mid-nineteenth century. But it must be remembered that Queen Victoria was essentially ruled by her emotions—she was capable of the most deep attachments and the most fervent antipathies; naturally, when stunned by grief, her response was exaggerated. She was also inclined to be manic depressive. Throughout the summer after the Duchess's death, Victoria began to regain her composure, though the opening of the newly-completed mausoleum, in August, reopened the wound:

We walked there after breakfast with Alice and Augusta B.—carrying the four pretty wreaths, and others of myrtle and immortelles; dear Papa [Albert] opened the gates, and we went into the vault which is so light and airy and nice and here we stood before the noble, granite sarcophagus on which and at the feet of which we placed the wreaths—and here we remained some few minutes. Tears flowed—but they were soothing, not those bitter, despairing ones—which I shed yesterday evening before dinner when I sat in those dear rooms full of everything she used and liked. But I got calmer and better—the night was good—and this morning on waking I felt quiet and calm and the impression left upon my mind of living in the dear sweet house is pleasing—not one of desolation. This afternoon we return to Osborne.[17]

Ever since those dark days in March, the Prince Consort had been the Queen's chief solace. Sharing in his wife's grief, soothing her in the moments of the worst distress, as well as showing his customary patience as she struggled to regain her spirits, brought Albert closer to Victoria than ever before. She relied on him completely and, in that summer and autumn after the Duchess of Kent's death, looked forward to many years in which to return his devotion and prove her own love for him. But Victoria was to be denied her years of happiness with her husband. In December of that fateful year, 1861, he too was taken from her by death. The loss of both mother and husband within such a short space of time was to deprive the Queen of her equanimity for years, and was to have no little effect on the course of English history.

When I set out to research this biography, I found that the material for it fell into four categories: contemporary matter —that is, newspaper and magazine accounts of the Duchess of Kent's actions, occasionally with criticism of them, published contemporaneously with events; the biographies of her daughter written between her accession in 1837 and her death in 1901; diaries, memoirs and correspondence of contemporaries in which the Duchess of Kent figures; and, finally, modern biographies which sift the evidence of the other three sources, and whose writers may have been so fortunate as to have access (denied to the present biographer) to the Duchess's and Queen Victoria's papers in the Royal Archives at Windsor.

The first phase, that of contemporary periodicals—begins with the preliminaries to the Kent marriage, then goes on with the glowing descriptions of the Duke's bride. Most of them dwell long on her relationship with the popular Prince Leopold and almost invariably misspell 'Leiningen'. But the ridicule which all public figures underwent in that era was also present: the royal brothers' pursuit of an heir to the kingdom was too ludicrous a situation for the Press to let pass without comment —and so, in April 1819, one cartoonist offends the Duchess's delicacy in alluding mischievously and graphically to her "interesting condition".

The death of the Duke of Kent in 1820 brought his widow momentarily into the limelight, and devotees of royalty might purchase for a small sum a poem, *Britannia's Tears*, by "a clergyman late of Oxford", in which the Duchess's virtues were extolled—and in which she is erroneously addressed as "Louisa":

> Ye friends of the helpless, yet patrons of truth,
> His benevolence imitate whose name you revere;
> Ye daughters of Britain, sweet guides of our youth,
> Let LOUISA'S bright beam your darkest night cheer.[18]

For the next decade, only occasional glimpses of the Duchess and her children can be gleaned, and those in the dry prose of the Court Circulars: "Yesterday the Duchess of Kent and the Princess Feodore visited the Duchess of Clarence"; or in descriptions of the gowns which the Duchess and her children wore to royal drawing-rooms. Only Parliament's granting of an additional income to the Duchess in 1825 brings any closer understanding of her situation.

Then, with the death of George IV, she is brought into focus, again the butt of critics and cartoonists in her bid for the regency; sharing their attacks with her brother Leopold, whose popularity had waned as he continued to draw his annuity of £50,000 from the nation, which began to notice that it got the minimum of return on its money. The accession of William IV also brought the child Victoria into the public eye, as heiress presumptive to the crown, and, since she was too closely guarded for much to be known of her, her mother was accorded the lion's share of the publicity. Most of it was harmless enough, and much of it praised her, but she might well have been annoyed at reading details of her relationship with her first husband:

> The disparity in age between them, was too great to secure even the probability of much conjugal felicity, for the bridegroom was twenty-eight years older than the bride. Nor was this all, if the voice of common rumour may be believed. The person, the manners, the qualifications, and the habits of the Prince of Leiningen, were little calculated to throw a veil over that disproportion of years which the hand of time had marked. Irritable and violent in temper, and solely devoted to the pleasures of the chase, his youthful consort could hardly hope to find in his society a compensation for the sacrifice which her filial feelings had prompted. But even at that early age, when passions are wildest, and the reason is all too weak to moderate them,

her Royal Highness gave evidence of that deep self-respect, which is the only secure basis of virtue.[19]

That extract from *The Royal Lady's Magazine* appeared in June 1831—an edifying piece about the mother of the heir to the throne, and an indication of the nature of the woman who might, at any moment, be called upon to realize the regency for her child. But only four months later, the same magazine felt it incumbent to take up the cudgels to protect the Duchess's good name against attacks on her insistence on not attending the coronation.

As the 1830s advanced, and the young Victoria was brought more into the public eye, touring England, the Press again reported the plain facts. Her mother's gracious replies to loyal addresses were reproduced fully in local newspapers, and occasionally in the national dailies. Not until 1837, when Victoria became Queen, was there any more opprobrium, and then it was of the usual xenophobic variety, more general than personal.

The Lady Flora Hastings scandal enjoyed full Press coverage. It was surely the forerunner in medium-treatment of the 'Profumo affair' of the early 1960s, throwing its net over the principals of the business and sending out wide ripples of rumour. Yet, in this case at least, the Duchess had but a small share in the scurrilities, the Hastings family grateful for her partisanship and the leader-writers concentrating on blackening the name of the Queen.

For the rest of her life, the Duchess of Kent played only a peripheral role in the Court, and none at all in politics: she was once again relegated to factual notices in the Court Circulars until her death, in March 1861, called forth glowing obituaries, which dwelt on her blameless moral education and character formation of her daughter.

Soon after the accession of Victoria, biographies flooded the market for the information of her subjects. As the reign advanced, anecdotes of her childhood came to light—the "I will be good" legend emerges. Invariably, her mother is praised: as one W. W. Tulloch wrote, ". . . the Princess was brought up entirely by her mother, who was everything that a kind, wise, and good mother ought to have been".[20] By the end of the reign there were dozens of versions of the Queen's life, both in magazines and in book form. All ignored the periods of criticism which the monarchy had suffered; none of them mentioned either her father's mistress or her mother's suspected liaison with Conroy—as often from ignorance as from delicacy; none of them implied anything but that the Queen enjoyed an idyllic childhood. Everywhere, the biographer's treatment of the Duchess of Kent was sympathetic and reverent. Thus, from 1840 until the publication of Lytton Strachey's deeper, better researched and more critical study of the Queen, in 1921, the character of the Duchess of Kent was held to be unimpeachable—with one exception.

This exception was the sensational publication of Henry Reeve's edition of the *Greville Memoirs* between 1874 and 1887. One has only to scan the Greville extracts of those editions used in this book to understand why Queen Victoria was so shocked on reading the memoirs: the diarist vaunted suspicions of her mother's adultery with Conroy, actually confirmed by the Duke of Wellington's opinion, when Victoria believed that no one outside the family circle had been aware of anything. There was King William's outburst at Windsor in 1836, word-for-word; Greville revealed Melbourne's indiscretions in describing to friends the strained relations between the Queen and her mother in 1837–40; the Lady Flora affair (though abbreviated from the original diary entries) was chronicled with relish; the ousting of Conroy was also sketched by the acid pen. The *Greville Memoirs* were a bombshell, though their editor had intended them merely to emphasize the Queen's own virtues through a contrast with the vices and foibles of her predecessors. (A fuller edition of 1938 expanded the more delicate areas of the *Memoirs*.)

Two years previously, the Queen had had a lesser shock with the appearance of the memoirs of Baron Stockmar, edited by his son, which showed the scope of Stockmar's influence on affairs which the public considered a purely British concern—though Stockmar, as the agent of the Coburgs, had only praise for the Queen's mother. In the 1880s, the *Posthumous Papers*

of Caroline Bauer were published; she had been Prince Leopold's mistress and was indiscreet enough to name members
of the Coburg family who had been among her acquaintances.
She it was who cited the letter from the Prince of Leiningen to
a lady of no reputation in which he condemned his wife's
family as promising him much and giving him nothing.

It was fortunate for Queen Victoria's sense of decorum that
the *Creevey Papers* did not appear until after her death
(1903–7), revealing as they did her father's long period of
domesticity with Julie St Laurent, his unhappiness at having
to contract a formal marriage and the gossip's criticism of his
manners and conduct. But memoirs and published correspondence are the vital ingredients of social history and biography,
and, fortunately for their victims, often highlight their good
qualities as well as prising skeletons from cupboards. The Queen
would approve wholeheartedly of the reminiscences of a childhood acquaintance, Jane Harriet Ellice, who described a meeting with the Duchess of Kent at Ramsgate in 1836: "The
strongest impression I brought away with me was the gracious,
smiling, gentle kindness of the Duchess of Kent, which always
seemed to shine in her face whenever we afterwards met."[21]
In 1927 came the publication of the *Letters of Lady Augusta
Stanley*, which served to enhance the reputation of the Duchess,
through the writer's obvious devotion to such a perfectly-
comported old lady, and by her insistence on the mutual
affection of the Queen and her mother.

The latest phase of the Duchess's handling by biographers
began in 1921 with Lytton Strachey's biography of Queen
Victoria. Unhampered by the awe and respect of his predecessors for their august subject, Strachey named Julie St
Laurent for the first time, and did not hesitate to name Conroy
too, with emphasis on the Queen's unhappy teenage years and
the period of coolness between her and her mother. He was
the first of the modern biographers of the Queen, with access
to much primary material, which by then included the published editions of the Queen's early letters (1908) and her
journal of 1832–40 (1912)—though they had been carefully
edited to exclude anything that might offend, including all

derogation of Conroy and any hint of the Lady Flora episode. Strachey's work was the definitive life of the Queen for many years, though the primary sources he had used were to be the meat of many lesser biographies. It was not until 1964 that Strachey was overtaken by a new study, the best-selling *Victoria R.I.* by Elizabeth Longford, a masterpiece in the art of biography, in which the author's access to the private papers of the royal family in the Windsor Archives brings to light many new facts, and gives opportunity for a revaluation of personalities and motives. Lady Longford's judgment is always objective and her arguments feasible; she is scrupulous in dealing with the character defects of Queen Victoria's mother, but clears her name once and for ever of the suspicion of adultery with Conroy:

> The Duchess's moral principles were genuine, as Queen Victoria realized as soon as she had emerged from the miasma of 1839. Amid the welter of remorse in which the Duchess indulged after the discovery of Conroy's dishonesty, she never wrote a word to suggest that she repented of anything but her own extreme carelessness, her blind trust in Conroy and his offensiveness to her daughter. The correspondence between the Duchess and the Queen must surely have taken a very different form had the Duchess been repenting of adultery. She would hardly have insisted up to the last that Conroy had been "very useful to her". Nor would Queen Victoria have wasted sympathy on her mother's 'shock' at his death.[22]

Other biographers have their own summation of Victoria, Duchess of Kent. In 1938, David Duff wrote:

> For the first seventeen years Queen Victoria's mother never left her child's side. During those years she followed her husband's last instructions to the letter—that she should be the sole guardian of their child. In so doing she suppressed her mother-love in order that her daughter might be trained with the firmness necessary to fit a child for the throne. As a result Victoria felt less love for her mother than for the visionary figure of the father she had never known. In her own words: "I am a soldier's daughter."[23]

In his *Youthful Queen Victoria*, of 1952, Dormer Creston described her mother as a chameleon, who suited her actions to the expectations of the men who dominated her—Edward, Leopold, Conroy and Albert, and decided that

> The way she blotted out all happiness from Feodore's young life and crushed Victoria; her bullying ingratitude to the kindly intentioned William and Adelaide choke any tender feelings that one might harbour for her; but, as one ponders on the ups and downs of an existence whose oscillations were certainly remarkable, one undeniably draws a good deal of entertainment from the spectacle. Four men in succession dominated her actions, and each, so it seems, for the time being dominated her mind as well.[24]

Ernest Raymond's judgment (1963) was that "The Duchess was a weak and foolish woman."[25]

Her own biographer, D. M. Stuart, to date the only writer to make a deep study of her as the central character of a work, did not attempt to analyse her subject, but wrote in the foreword (to *Mother of Victoria*, 1941): ". . . the Duchess presents quite a pretty psychological problem of the 'double-personality' order, for before 1829 and after 1840 we look in vain for this arrogant intransigent Princess, finding in her stead only, as the Queen wrote later, 'the gentlest creature one can ever imagine'."[26]

More than a year ago, I set out to find out about Queen Victoria's mother. Once I knew who she was and what she did, I began to probe her motives; to examine the extent of her power to control her own destiny; and then to assess her character and personality. In libraries and archives in London and Oxford, I read what observers and friends had written about her; in Germany, I saw rooms in which she had lived, and gardens in which she had walked. When I came to write this book, after months of research, I was surprised to find how well I had come to know a woman who had died over a century ago.

Victoire lived at a time, and was born to a position, which ruled that her life must be controlled by elders and superiors, and by 'duty'. When she was under that personal control, as she was for the first thirty-five years of her life, she was submissive and unremarkable. Only when she found that power over her own destiny and that of her child lay in her own hands did she falter. Is it therefore surprising that the Duchess of Kent made mistakes? Is it surprising that she was swayed by more forceful personalities—that she fell for the persuasions of Conroy and finally yielded to the strong-minded Queen Victoria? Only when the Duchess of Kent was once more on the safe ground of the familiar submission of a minor role cast for her by others did she regain her balance. Her mistakes are so understandable as to be almost inevitable.

The Duchess of Kent was neither 'good' nor 'bad', neither genius nor simpleton. She lived her life as it came from Providence; she tried to make the best of it, to fulfil the potential she believed she possessed; when chance of power and fame was denied her, she came cheerfully to terms with obscurity; she was loved by many and disliked by comparatively few. How many of us would despise such a fate for ourselves?

NOTES TO CHAPTER TEN

1 Queen Victoria to Leopold, King of the Belgians, 25.5.59: Benson and Esher (ed.), *Letters of Queen Victoria*, volume iii, p. 335.

2 *Ibid.*, 7.8.60: *Ibid.*, volume iii, p. 406.

3 Albert, Prince Consort, to Victoria, Duchess of Kent, 10.2.61: Jagow (ed.), *Letters of the Prince Consort*, p. 359.

4 Lady Augusta Bruce to Lady Frances Baillie, 7.3.61: Bolitho and Baillie (ed.), *Letters of Lady Augusta Stanley, 1849–63*, p. 184.

5 *Ibid.*, 6.4.61: *Ibid.*, p. 193.

6 *Ibid.*

7 *Ibid.*, p. 197–8.

8 Queen Victoria to Leopold, King of the Belgians, 16.3.61: Benson and Esher, *op. cit.*, volume iii, p. 435.

9 George, fourth Earl of Clarendon to Louise, Duchess of Manchester, 25.12.61: Kennedy (ed.), *My Dear Duchess*, p. 207.

10 Queen Victoria to Leopold, King of the Belgians, 26.3.61: Benson and Esher (ed.), *op. cit.*, volume iii, p. 436.

11 Queen Victoria to Princess Victoria of Prussia, 10.4.61: Fulford (ed.), *Dearest Child*, pp. 319–20.

12 Reeve (ed.), *Greville Memoirs*, volume iv, p. 364: 27.3.61.
13 *Lady's Pocket Magazine*, July 1832, volume i, p. 106–7.
14 Lady Augusta Stanley to Queen Victoria, 19.8.74: Bolitho and Baillie (ed.), *Later Letters of Lady Augusta Stanley*, pp. 255–6.
15 Queen Victoria to Leopold, King of the Belgians, 9.4.61: Benson and Esher (ed.), *op. cit.*, volume iii, p. 439.
16 Pope-Hennessy, *Agnes Strickland*, p. 267.
17 Queen Victoria to Princess Victoria of Prussia, 17.8.61: Fulford (ed.), *op. cit.*, pp. 343–4.
18 *Britannia's Tears*, p. 16.
19 *Royal Lady's Magazine*, June 1831, volume i, p. 368.
20 Tulloch, *Story of the Life of Queen Victoria*, p. 6.
21 Ellice, 'Some memories of the Queen's childhood and marriage', *Cornhill Magazine*, June 1897.
22 Longford, *Victoria R.I.*, p. 148.
23 Duff, *Edward of Kent*, p. 295.
24 Creston, *Youthful Queen Victoria*, p. 454.
25 Raymond (ed.), *Queen Victoria's Early Letters*, p. 3.
26 Stuart, *Mother of Victoria*, pp. vii–viii.

GENEALOGICAL TABLES

Queen Victoria's Maternal Relations

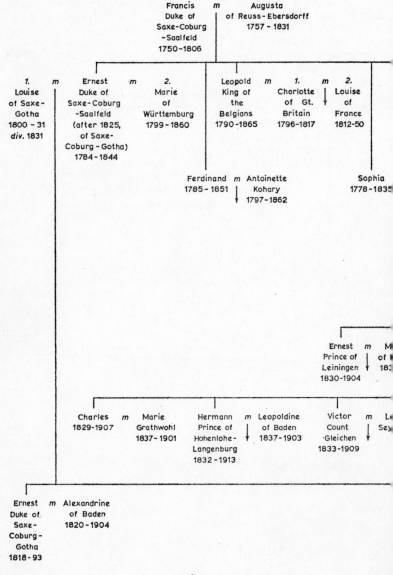

Francis
Duke of
Saxe-Coburg
-Saalfeld
1750-1806

m

Augusta
of Reuss-Ebersdorff
1757 - 1831

1. *m*	Ernest *m*	*2.*	Leopold *m*	*1.* *m*	*2.*		
Louise	Duke of	Marie	King of	Charlotte	Louise		
of Saxe-	Saxe-Coburg	of	the	of Gt.	of		
Gotha	-Saalfeld	Württemburg	Belgians	Britain	France		
1800 - 31	(after 1825,	1799-1860	1790-1865	1796-1817	1812-50		
div. 1831	of Saxe-						
	Coburg-Gotha)						
	1784-1844						

Ferdinand *m* Antoinette
1785-1851 | Kohary
1797-1862

Sophia
1778-1835

Ernest *m* M
Prince of | of ▮
Leiningen ▼ 18▮
1830-1904

Charles *m* Marie
1829-1907 Grathwohl
1837-1901

Hermann *m* Leopoldine
Prince of | of Baden
Hohenlohe- ▼ 1837-1903
Langenburg
1832-1913

Victor *m* L▮
Count | Se▮
·Gleichen ▼
1833-1909

Ernest *m* Alexandrine
Duke of. of Baden
Saxe- 1820-1904
Coburg-
Gotha
1818-93

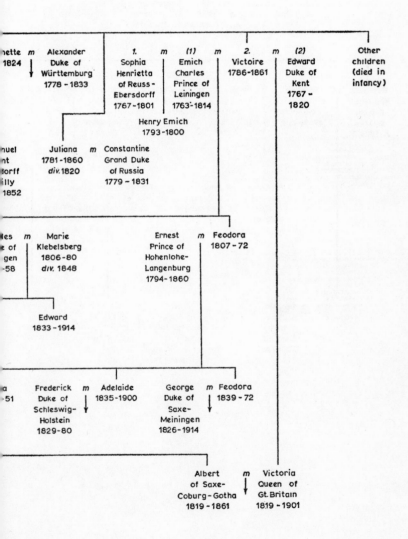

hette *m* Alexander
1824   Duke of
Württemburg
1778 – 1833

1.   *m*   (1)   *m*   2.   *m*   (2)   Other
Sophia   Emich   Victoire   Edward   children
Henrietta   Charles   1786-1861   Duke of   (died in
of Reuss-   Prince of   Kent   infancy)
Ebersdorff   Leiningen   1767 –
1767-1801   1763-1814   1820

Henry Emich
1793-1800

nuel   Juliana   *m*   Constantine
nt   1781-1860   Grand Duke
dorff   *div.* 1820   of Russia
illy   1779 – 1831
1852

les   *m*   Marie   Ernest   *m*   Feodora
of   Klebelsberg   Prince of   1807 – 72
gen   1806-80   Hohenlohe-
-58   *div.* 1848   Langenburg
                          1794-1860

Edward
1833-1914

a   Frederick   *m*   Adelaide   George   *m*   Feodora
-51   Duke of   1835-1900   Duke of   1839 – 72
Schleswig-   Saxe-
Holstein   Meiningen
1829-80   1826-1914

Albert   *m*   Victoria
of Saxe-   Queen of
Coburg-Gotha   Gt. Britain
1819 – 1861   1819 – 1901

L

Queen Victoria's Paternal Relations

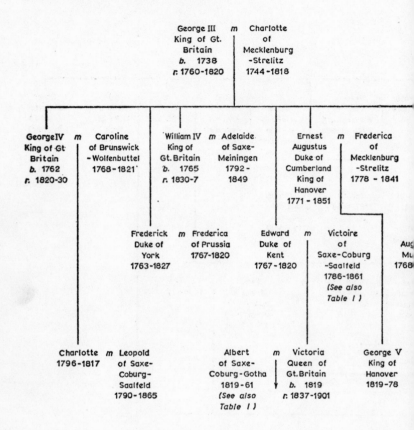

George III m Charlotte
King of Gt. of
Britain Mecklenburg
b. 1738 -Strelitz
r. 1760-1820 1744-1818

GeorgeIV m Caroline
King of Gt of Brunswick
Britain -Wolfenbuttel
b. 1762 1768-1821
r. 1820-30

William IV m Adelaide
King of of Saxe-
Gt.Britain Meiningen
b. 1765 1792-
r. 1830-7 1849

Ernest m Frederica
Augustus of
Duke of Mecklenburg
Cumberland -Strelitz
King of 1778 - 1841
Hanover
1771 - 1851

Frederick m Frederica
Duke of of Prussia
York 1767-1820
1763-1827

Edward m Victoire
Duke of of
Kent Saxe-Coburg
1767-1820 -Saalfeld
1786-1861
(See also
Table I)

Aug
Mu
1768

Charlotte m Leopold
1796-1817 of Saxe-
Coburg-
Saalfeld
1790-1865

Albert m Victoria
of Saxe- Queen of
Coburg-Gotha Gt.Britain
1819-61 b. 1819
(See also r. 1837-1901
Table I)

George V
King of
Hanover
1819-78

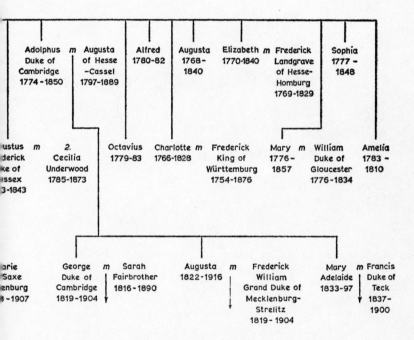

Adolphus _m_ Augusta | Alfred | Augusta | Elizabeth _m_ Frederick | Sophia
Duke of   of Hesse   1780-82   1768-   1770-1840   Landgrave   1777 -
Cambridge -Cassel   1840   of Hesse-   1848
1774 -1850 1797-1889   Homburg
                                                          1769-1829

ustus _m_ 2.   Octavius Charlotte _m_ Frederick   Mary _m_ William   Amelia
derick   Cecilia   1779-83   1766-1828   King of   1776 -   Duke of   1783 -
ke of   Underwood   Württemburg   1857   Gloucester 1810
ssex   1785-1873   1754-1876   1776 -1834
3-1843

arie   George _m_ Sarah   Augusta _m_ Frederick   Mary _m_ Francis
Saxe   Duke of   Fairbrother 1822-1916   William   Adelaide   Duke of
enburg   Cambridge 1816-1890   Grand Duke of   1833-97   Teck
3-1907   1819-1904   Mecklenburg-   1837-
                                               Strelitz   1900
                                               1819 - 1904

163

BIBLIOGRAPHY

BIOGRAPHIES

Albert, H. A., *Queen Victoria's Sister* (Robert Hale, 1967)
Anonymous, *Alice* (John Murray, 1884)
Bolitho, H., *A Biographer's Notebook* (Longmans Green, 1950)
—— *Albert, Prince Consort* (David Bruce & Watson, 1970)
Campbell, John, Duke of Argyll, *V.R.I.* (Eyre & Spottiswood, 1902)
Corti, E. (J. McCabe, trans.), *Leopold I of Belgium* (T. Fisher Unwin, 1923)
Creston, D., *The Youthful Queen Victoria* (Macmillan, 1952)
D'Auvergne, E. B., *The Coburgs* (Stanley Paul, 1911)
Duff, D., *Edward of Kent* (Stanley Paul, 1938)
—— *Victoria Travels* (Muller, 1970)
Firth, D., *The Case of Augustus d'Este* (Cambridge University Press, 1948)
Fulford, R., *The Prince Consort* (Macmillan, 1949)
—— *Royal Dukes* (Duckworth, 1933)
Gillen, M., *The Prince and his Lady* (Sidgwick & Jackson, 1970)
Grey, C., *Early Life of the Prince Consort* (1867)
Gurney, D. F., *The Childhood of Queen Victoria* (J. Nisbet, 1901)
Hopkirk, M., *Queen Adelaide* (John Murray, 1946)
Jerrold, C., *The Early Court of Queen Victoria* (Eveleigh Nash, 1912)
Lancaster, O., 'Tragedy at Claremont' in *Cornhill Magazine*, 1937
Longford, E., *Victoria R.I.* (Weidenfeld & Nicolson, 1964)
Neale, E., *The Life of H.R.H. Edward, Duke of Kent* (1850)
Pope-Hennessey, U., *Agnes Strickland* (Chatto & Windus, 1940)
Porter, M., *Overture to Victoria* (Alvin Redman, 1961)
Richardson, J., *My Dearest Uncle* (Jonathan Cape, 1961)
Strachey, L., *Queen Victoria* (Chatto & Windus, 1921)
Stuart, D. M., *Mother of Victoria* (Macmillan, 1941)
—— *Daughters of George III* (Macmillan, 1939)
Tulloch, W. W., *The Story of the Life of Queen Victoria* (J. Nisbet, 1901)

CORRESPONDENCE, MEMOIRS, DIARIES ETC.

Albert, Prince (K. von Jagow, ed.) *Letters of the Prince Consort, 1831–61* (John Murray, 1938)

Ashton, J., *Gossip in the First Decade of Victoria's Reign* (Hurst & Blackett, 1903)

Augusta, Dowager Duchess of Saxe-Coburg-Saalfeld (Princess Beatrice, ed.), *In Napoleonic Days* (John Murray, 1941)

Bauer, Caroline (C. Nisbet, ed.), *Caroline Bauer and the Coburgs* (Vizetelly & Co., 1885)

Buckingham, Duke of, *Memoirs of the Court of England during the Regency, 1811–20* (Hurst & Blackett, 1861)

Cathcart, H., *A Royal Bedside Book* (W. H. Allen, 1969)

Creevey, Thomas (Sir H. Maxwell, ed.), *Creevey Papers* (John Murray, 1904)

Croker (L. J. Jennings, ed.), *Croker Papers*

Dino, Dorothea, Duchess of, *Memoirs* (Heinemann, 1908)

George, Prince of Wales (A. Aspinall, ed.), *Correspondence of George, Prince of Wales, 1770–1812* (Cambridge University Press, 1963)

—— *Letters of George IV, 1812–30* (Cambridge University Press, 1938)

Greville, Charles Cavendish Fulke (R. Fulford and L. Strachey, ed.), *Greville Memoirs* (Macmillan, 1938)

—— (H. Reeve, ed.), *Greville Memoirs* (Longmans Green, 1874–87)

Jerningham (E. Castle, ed.), *Jerningham Letters* (1896)

Lieven, Princess (G. le Strange, ed.), *Correspondence of Princess Lieven and Earl Grey* (Bentley & Son, 1890)

—— (P. Quennell, ed.), *Private Letters of Princess Lieven to Prince Metternich, 1820–6* (John Murray, 1937)

—— (L. G. Robinson, ed.), *Letters of Dorothea, Princess Lieven during her residence in London, 1812–34* (Longmans Green, 1902)

—— (Lord Sudley, ed.), *Palmerston-Lieven Correspondence, 1828–58* (John Murray, 1943)

—— (H. Temperley, ed.), *Unpublished Diary. . . .* (Jonathan Cape, 1925)

Lindsay, P., *Recollections of a Royal Parish* (John Murray, 1902)

Locker-Lampson, F., *My Confidences* (Smith Elder, 1896)

Lyttelton, Lady (H. Wyndham, ed.), *Correspondence of Sarah Spencer, Lady Lyttelton, 1787–1870* (John Murray, 1912)

Manchester, Louise, Duchess of (A. Kennedy, ed.), *My Dear Duchess* (John Murray, 1956)

Marie Louise, H.R.H. Princess, *My Memories of Six Reigns* (Evans Bros, 1956)

Owen, R., *Life of Robert Owen* (Wilson, 1837–8)

Stanley, Lady Augusta (H. Bolitho and W. Baillie, ed.), *Letters of Lady Augusta Stanley, 1849–63* (Howe, 1927)
—— (H. Bolitho and W. Baillie, ed.), *Later Letters of Lady Augusta Stanley, 1864–76* (Jonathan Cape, 1929)
Stockmar, Baron (E. Stockmar, ed., M. Muller, trans.), *Memoirs of Baron Stockmar* (Longmans Green, 1872)
Victoria, H.M. Queen (H. Bolitho, ed.), *Further Letters of Queen Victoria* (Thorton-Butterworth, 1938)
—— (Viscount Esher, ed.), *The Girlhood of Queen Victoria* (John Murray, 1912)
—— (Viscount Esher and A. C. Benson, ed.), *The Letters of Queen Victoria, 1826–61*, first series (John Murray, 1907)
—— (R. Fulford, ed.), *Dearest Child* (Evans Bros, 1965)
—— (J. Raymond, ed.), *The Early Letters of Queen Victoria* (Batsford, 1963)
Wellington, first Duke of (G. Wellesley, Duke of Wellington, ed.), *A Selection from the Private Correspondence of the first Duke of Wellington* (Roxburghe Club, 1952)
Wilberforce, W., *Diary*

FOREIGN WORKS

J. P. L. E. Brinckmeier, *Genealogische Geschichte . . . Hauses Leiningen etc* (Sattler, Brunswick, 1890)
M. Walter, *Die Kunstbestrebungen des Furstenhauses Leiningen im 19 Jahrhundert* (Freunde Mainfrankischer Kunst und Geschichte E. V., Wurzburg, 1950)

UNPUBLISHED MATERIAL

Sir John Conroy's family papers in Balliol College, Oxford
MS of Lord Augustus d'Este's memoranda of his health in the Royal College of Physicians, London

CONTEMPORARY NEWSPAPERS, MAGAZINES AND PAMPHLETS

Morning Chronicle
Morning Herald
Morning Post
The Times

BIBLIOGRAPHY

The *Gentleman's Magazine*
La Belle Assemblée
The *Lady's Magazine*
The *Lady's Monthly Museum*
The *Lady's Pocket Magazine*
The *Royal Lady's Magazine*
The *Window of Fashion*

Almanach de Gotha
Britannia's Tears, 'A clergyman late of Oxford' (1820)
A Diary of Royal Movements, volume i, 1819–46 (1883)
The *Double Bereavement* (1820)
Victim of Scandal (1839)

INDEX